listen to her voice

Listen deep into their stories for their voices. . . .
They live in the spaces between the words, men's
words, but in the spaces you will hear them tell a
different story. If you have the heart to hear.

—Peter Pitzele, *Our Fathers' Wells*

listen to her voice

WOMEN OF THE HEBREW BIBLE

Miki Raver

CHRONICLE BOOKS
SAN FRANCISCO

First Chronicle Books LLC paperback edition, published in 2005.

Pages 170–174 constitute a continuation of the copyright page.

ISBN 0-8118-4747-0

The Library of Congress has cataloged the previous edition as follows:
  Raver, Miki.
    Listen to her voice : women of the Hebrew Bible / by Miki Raver.
        p.   cm.
    Includes bibliographical references and index.
    ISBN 0-8118-1895-0 (hc)
    1. Women in the Bible—Biography. 2. Bible. O.T.—Biography.
    3. Feminism—Religious aspects—Judaism. 4. Judaism—Doctrines. I. Title.
  BS575.R38 1997
  221.9'2'082—dc21   97-49312
                            CIP

Manufactured in China.

Design by Pamela Geismar
Calligraphy by Naomi Teplow
Composition by Neal Elkin, On Line Typography

Distributed in Canada by Raincoast Books
9050 Shaughnessy Street
Vancouver, BC V6P 6E5

10 9 8 7 6 5 4 3 2 1

Chronicle Books LLC
85 Second Street
San Francisco, CA 94105

www.chroniclebooks.com

page 2: Sir Edward Burne-Jones, *The Days of Creation: The Sixth Day: Creation of Adam and Eve*

To Sasha, my mother, and Sasha, my daughter.

contents

	Foreword	8
	Introduction	11
Genesis	EVE	16
	SARAH	26
	REBECCA	40
	RACHEL & LEAH	54
	DINA	68
	TAMAR	74
Exodus & Numbers	MIRIAM	82
Judges	DEBORAH	92
	DELILAH	100
1 Samuel	HANNAH	106
	ABIGAIL	112
2 Samuel & 1 Kings	BATHSHEBA	118
1 Kings & 2 Kings	QUEEN OF SHEBA	126
	JEZEBEL	132
The Writings	RUTH & NAOMI	140
	ESTHER	150
	Acknowledgments	164
	Endnotes	166
	Bibliography	167
	List of Illustrations	170
	Bible Acknowledgments	174

FOREWORD
a woman's voice
by Rabbi Lynn Gottlieb

Miriam plays the timbrel and waters part.
Her sisters dance and the sea skips aside.
Waves crash to thunderous music.
Rousing jubilations
hallow the gift of Hebrew liberation.
To be free is what women sing.

Miki Raver is a modern day Miriam
singing the songs of her Biblical sisters,
thickening the interpretive canvas of their stories,
liberating their names from the margins of silence
in her own soul.
She discovers their voices
by reading them against the text
of her own life.

The names of Biblical women are not unfamiliar.
The names of our Biblical mothers
form the marrow in our bones.
Hava, Ruth, Naomi.
Names we inhabit in our bedrooms and kitchens,
names we move across oceans with our breath.
Sarah, Hannah, Avigayal.
Names we choose for our daughters

in honor of a great grandmother from the
old country
who never walked more than five miles from her
native village
and cried when she found out the world
was not flat.
Dinah, Batsheva, Esther.
Names that call us to Torah,
names that collect memories,
names that make us relatives.
Devorah, Yael, Tamar.
Names of distant cousins who show up every year
for the family Passover,
names of girls we share a cabin with at Jewish
summer camp,
names of Israelis who ride the bus to Tel Aviv,
names of women in our Rosh Chodesh circle and
members of Hadassah.
Rivkeh, Rahel, and Leah.
We use their recipes to bake our holy day breads,
their language to bless and curse,
their rhythms to deepen our joy.
Our fierceness for survival is inherited
from the original bearers of these names,
desert women,
who knew how to consecrate an enduring flame.

The names of our Biblical mothers
summon us to remember our roots.
In this generation new growth
stirs within this ancient tree of names.
Women are reauthoring the past,
pruning deadly motifs,
cutting away stale conventions
that suspend our lives
between fixed poles of virtue and vilification.
Behold! New branches
are emerging on the vine.
Delilah, Jezebel, and the Queen of Sheba.
This generation of women chooses
to hear the story of women
whose independence made them suspect,
whose strategy for survival condemned them
as enemies,
whose foreignness doomed them to an
unsympathetic read.
This generation of women reclaims
the totality of women's wisdom, rage,
and point of view.
No longer will our sexuality be an
interpretive weapon
against our own lives.
No longer will we be divided
from sisters whose struggle is mirrored in our own.

Listen to Her Voice
is a *midrashic* act
illuminated by a host of inquiries,
linguistic analyses, cross cultural comparisons,
anthropological investigations, artistic viewpoints,
previous Rabbinic commentaries,
and contemporary women's scholarship.
Yet, as Miki Raver writes in her concluding
commentary,
"love is the redemptive force" in these stories.
Miki's love of her Jewish self,
born in the graceful kindling of Sabbath light,
is sustained and enhanced in her rendering of these
sacred tales.
May we be inspired by her voice
to look anew at women's lives
and find within them old stories
and new songs of joy.

introduction

As a little girl, I watched my mother light candles on Friday nights. Her hands circled the flames three times, as she gathered the light to her heart. I have been drawn to the flame of Judaism, gathering its light to my heart, ever since.

Most of my community of friends, born into Jewish and Christian traditions, have embraced the spiritual practices of Buddhism, Hinduism, or Taoism. The spiritual path that enriches my life is Judaism. Friends come to our house to celebrate the Sabbath and Jewish holidays. Each Friday night, we say blessings over candles, bread, and wine. We eat apples dipped in honey to celebrate a sweet New Year and cast crumbs of bread, symbols of our sins, into waters that run to the sea. On Chanukah, we devour potato latkes, light the menorah, and give gifts. On Passover, I lead a seder, tambourine in hand. We sing, feast, and tell the story of our people's liberation from slavery. My life has been defined and embellished by these occasions.

In preparation for these holy days, I have learned about the ritual, philosophy, and history of my people. I am self-taught and my observation of Jewish religious tradition is individualistic. Because I was a girl and joining a temple would have strained my family's budget, I never went to Hebrew school. Perhaps that is one reason I love a religion so many of my contemporaries in the tribe shun. Hebrew schools in the 1950s were not known for sparking spiritual connection. Fearing that institutionalized Judaism could dim the light of this spiritual path for me, I have always been Jewish in a way that feels meaningful to me, listening to my inner voice, observing those rituals that nourish my soul.

Witnessing the Torah (the first five books of the Hebrew Bible, perfectly inscribed by hand on a parchment scroll) being taken from the ark—

Abel Pann
Genesis 30:22, "Elohim remembered Rachel" (detail)

and lovingly paraded around the sanctuary—has always moved me to tears. But like most assimilated Jews of my generation, I distanced myself from the Bible. I knew I should read it, but I procrastinated, thinking that it would be a bore, sure that I'd be irritated by the patriarchal bias I'd heard so much about.

I needed to find a path into the Bible text, so I decided to begin by reading only the stories of the women, specifically those women whose names I recognized. Daughters have been named after biblical women for thousands of years. My daughter, Sara, is. Everyone knows a woman with one of these names. Most of us have loved someone with one of these names. I knew there must be a reason these ancient names had lived on from generation to generation. So I decided to read the stories of eighteen women of the Bible whose names are eternal. The number eighteen symbolizes life in Jewish mysticism. The stories of these women—Eve, Sarah, Rebecca, Rachel, Leah, Dina, Tamar, Miriam, Deborah, Delilah, Hannah, Abigail, Bathsheba, Queen of Sheba, Jezebel, Ruth, Naomi, Esther—brought the Bible vibrantly to life for me.

I bought a pocket edition of The New Jerusalem Bible, the only Bible I could find that had an index of names. I carried it everywhere, reading the women's tales while commuting, waiting for jury duty, sunbathing on Northern California beaches. I felt sure people thought I was an obsessed fundamentalist as I avidly read my pocket Bible. Sometimes I reacted audibly, commenting or gasping at what I was reading. Often, I could not believe my eyes. I was gripped, shocked, and deeply fascinated. Bored I was not. The texts of these surprisingly sexual, often violent stories are highly provocative. These aren't sweet stories about nice little women. Our foremothers were strong, independent, rebellious, courageous, and real. Their issues remain—infertility and surrogate motherhood, infidelity and jealousy, incest and rape. Their lives, like ours, were about the dance of opposites: sacrifice and fulfillment, acceptance and rejection, longing and liberation.

I could feel the power of these women. I could feel their heat. Sexuality, spirituality, and strategy were the themes of their tales. The Bible text was powerful but cryptic. I had to read between the lines, allowing my imagination to illuminate the text. I questioned, analyzed, and opined. The more I questioned, the deeper I went.

At first I felt guilty about applying my rebellious, contemporary perspective to the holy text. Now I know that I was creating midrash and following age-old tradition. Midrash is the interpretation and commentary that emerges from questioning what's written in the Bible. It springs from the Hebrew word *l'drash,* meaning "to question." The Torah is layered with many levels of understanding, each word holding a vast number of meanings, all of which are true. The interpretive process is what gives the Bible its vitality and makes it a living, giving vessel.

For thousands of years, classic rabbinic midrash was created by men in study houses, while the women took care of the children and ran the family businesses. As a result, we have a highly respected body of interpretive literature that comes from an entirely male perspective, often reflecting a fear of the feminine and an investment in suppression of women. It was actually written in the Jerusalem Talmud that "the words of the Torah should be burnt rather than be taught to women." Blessedly, the golden age of feminism in the past three decades has brought a flourishing of midrash created by women. Women are adding compelling scholarly, psychological, and literary perspectives to Torah. So long excluded, we are finally taking our place.

The sages taught that the Bible is written with Black Fire on White Fire. The Black Fire is the text on the page. The White Fire is the space between the lines. It is in these holes that the holiness often resides. The White Fire is midrash, interpretation of the text. The Black Fire, rising like flames, like sparks in a vortex, rising to Heaven, contains messages for us all. The Bible has subtext of astonishing depth. There's meaning to be mined beneath the surface.

The Black Fire for this book could have come from any of numerous Bible translations, but none felt quite right. All used the pronoun "He," and "God" and "Lord" for the Divine, and that was unacceptable to me. As I read the women's stories in different versions of the Scripture, the word that worked best for me would vary from passage to passage. So with deepest sincerity, reverence, and awe, I chose the Bible text for this book, word for word and verse by verse by consulting eleven wonderful English Bible translations. The King James Version was the work of four hundred and fifty learned men in the 1600s. The New Jerusalem Bible, the accomplishment of a team of French Jesuits, reads like a juicy novel. The modern Jewish translations—Rabbi Aryeh Kaplan's *The Living Torah,* The Jewish Publication Society's Tanakh, Everett Fox's *The Five Books of Moses*—all powerfully convey Hebrew idiom and soul. Robert Alter's *Genesis* is inspiring and illuminating. Howard Bloom and David Rosenberg's *Book of J* is raw, brilliant poetry. The New American Standard, New Revised Standard, and Amplified translations are refreshingly clear. Yet sometimes all the existing texts used sexist language, and I would substitute my own. Although in ancient days, these stories were told by storytellers in women's circles, no woman's translation of the Hebrew Scripture yet exists. In the process of choosing Bible text, I discovered that all translation is interpretation and that verse thirteen almost always brings a plot twist.

My intention was to be true to the text, while using accessible, descriptive, and nonsexist words to tell these amazing stories. In bringing a woman's sensibility to the compilation, I eliminated all-male genealogy and added the foremothers' names to those of the forefathers in some passages. An ellipsis indicates a break in the text.

In the Torah, two names are usually used for the Divine. One is Elohim, which was translated to English as "God." The name is actually plural in the original Hebrew; it means "powers" and encompasses both feminine and masculine genders. Through the years, it was almost forgotten that the name Elohim has both masculine and feminine sides. The Divine began to be thought of as singular and male. This was a distortion of the theology of monotheism. We must remember that the word *Elohim* is plural, both Goddess and God, encompassing all. Goddess may seem like a less valid translation for *Elohim* than God, but its use feels uncomfortable simply because it's not traditional. It's unfamiliar because the feminine face of the Divine has been hidden for so long. If we accept Goddess as fully equal to God, the female aspect of the Holy One, then the time has come to say the word. But Goddess, like God, offers only a partial picture. To name the Divine in the Black Fire, I use Elohim. As for translation into English, I leave that to the reader.

Four Hebrew letters also name the Divine: *Yud, Hay, Vav, Hay.* Known as the Tetragrammaton, *YHVH* is a word without gender. It isn't a noun. It is the dynamic form of the verb "to be." When Moses asked the Holy One for a name to tell the people of Israel, the Divine reply was "I am that I am." There's momentous teaching in these words. Most English Bibles translate YHVH as Lord, which conjures a man as Master. Some Christian Bible translations use the words *Yahweh* or *Jehovah*. But traditional Judaism forbids the articulation of YHVH; in ancient times, YHVH was only pronounced by the High Priest, alone in the Holy of Holies (the innermost sanctum of the Jerusalem temple) on Yom Kippur. Today, the actual pronunciation has been lost. *Adonai* is almost always used in prayer but very rarely in Scripture. Ultimately, I decided to use Yah, a name for the Divine that the Jewish Renewal movement has adopted because it expresses the breath that gives us life and connects us with the Divine. I like how I feel when I say it. Its sound is ancient. To say it is heart-opening.

When the pronoun "He" was used in the Bible to name the Divine I substituted "Infinite One." It is a more accurate description of the ineffable. "He" is singular, masculine, and paints only half the picture. For thousands of years, the Divine carried only masculine names: God, never Goddess; He, never She. Until now. There has been a passionate turning toward the Divine Feminine in recent years. We have entered the new millennium on the wings of Shekhina.

The White Fire is a synthesis of my research and viewpoint. In my journey of discovery through the women's stories in the Bible, I found the Bible to be animated by the Divine Feminine and a tradition that honors women's strength, spirituality, and sexuality. This journey gifted me with my ancestresses as spirit guides.

Bring the warmth of your own White Fire to the Black Fire, your unique interpretation to the Scripture. The Bible holds infinite potential for meaning. To read the Bible is to enter a process. Wrestle with the text. Wrestle with the Divine. Question. The Kabbalah teaches that all the characters of the Torah are within ourselves. Brought to life with reading, interpretation, and meditation, our souls listen and our foremothers speak.

Miki Raver
Oakland, California

"Life-Giver"

EVE

Chavah

GENESIS : CHAPTER 1

26 And Yah Elohim said, "Let us make a human in our image, after our likeness . . . 27 And Elohim created the human in the image of the Infinite One, male and female the Infinite One created them.

GENESIS : CHAPTER 2

5 Now no plant of the field or herb of the earth had yet sprouted, for there was not yet rain, nor was there anyone to till the soil. 6 But a mist would rise up from the earth, and water the whole face of the ground. 7 And Yah Elohim formed a human from the clay of the earth and blew the spirit of life into its nostrils, and the human became a living soul.

8 And Yah Elohim made a garden grow eastward in Eden; and put the human there. 9 Out of the ground Yah Elohim made every tree that is pleasant to the sight and good to eat. In the middle of this garden were the Tree of Life and the Tree of Knowing Good and Evil.

15 Yah Elohim put the human in the Garden of Eden to cultivate and care for it. 16 And Yah Elohim instructed, "You may eat freely of all the trees of the garden. 17 But you must not eat from the Tree of Knowing Good and Evil; for the day you eat from it, you shall die!"

18 "It is not good for the human to be alone," said Yah Elohim. "I will make a partner for the human." 19 Now Yah Elohim had formed, out of the earth, all the animals of the field and all the birds of the sky, and brought each of them to the human to name. 20 The human gave names to all the animals of the field, the birds of the sky and the wild beasts. But none were a suitable partner for the human being. 21 So Yah Elohim made the human fall into a deep trance, and while the human slept, took a part from its side and closed up the flesh again. 22 From the human's side Yah Elohim built a woman and brought her to the man.

23 And Adam said, "This one at last is bone of my bones, and flesh of my flesh. Woman I call her, because she is part of man." 24 This is why a man leaves his mother and father and clings to his wife and they become one flesh.

25 They were naked, the man and the woman, and they felt no shame.

Andrea del Minga, *Creation of Eve* (detail)

say you're not allowed to eat from any tre
the garden?" the serpent asked the woma

2 She replied, "We may eat freely from
the garden. 3 But of the fruit from t
middle of the garden, Elohim said
eat it or even touch it, or you w

4 "Death will not touch you,"
woman. 5 "For Elohim kno
you eat from it, your eyes
will be like divine being

6 The woman saw ho
eyes and lively to t
fruit she reached
was with her, a
of them were
naked. So t
themselve

8 They
even
El

n
ta
Ot
and
all th
15 I w
and be
They sh
and you

16 The In
"Pain incre
in pain you
Your yearnin
and he will r

17 The Infinite
"Because you li
tree though I co
cursed be the soi

the fruit of the tree, and I ate."

13 "What is this you have done?" said Yah Elohim to the woman.

"The smooth-tongued snake beguiled me, and I ate."

14 Then Yah Elohim said to the snake:
'Because you have done this,
ore cursed are you than all animals wild and
me.
your belly you will go
dust you shall eat
e days of your life.
ill put enmity between you and the woman,
tween your offspring and hers.
all strike at your head,
shall strike at their heel."

inite One told the woman:
asing, groans that spread into groans,
shall give birth.
g will be for your husband,
le over you."

One said to Adam:
tened to her voice and ate from the
mmanded you, 'Do not eat from it,'
because of you.

Painfully will you get your food from it, all the days of your life.
18 It will yield you brambles and thistles,
as you eat the plants of the field.
19 By the sweat of your face
will you get your food,
until you return to the earth,
for from it you were taken.
For dust you are,
and to dust you shall return."

20 Then the man named the woman Eve (Life-Giver) because she was the mother of all who live.

21 Yah Elohim made garments of the skins of wild animals for the woman and man and clothed them. 22 Then Yah Elohim said, "The human beings have become like one of us, knowing good and evil. Now they must not be allowed to reach out and take also from the Tree of Life and eat, and live forever."

23 So Yah Elohim sent them away from the Garden of Eden, to toil in the earth from which they were taken. 24 East of Eden, the Infinite One posted two winged Cherubim and a fiery, flashing sword, turning in every direction, to guard the way to the Tree of Life. ◎◎

E V E was our living link with the Divine Feminine: "In Elohim's own image, male and female, did Elohim create them." (Genesis 1:27) The Bible began with a powerful acknowledgment of both feminine and masculine aspects of the Divine. We must always remember that Elohim is a plural noun, Goddess and God together, the feminine and masculine joined to form the Infinite One. But by the second chapter of the Bible, Elohim, called "God" in English translation, was thought of as singular and male. When Eve did not obey "Him," she was cursed with male domination. And the Goddess shared Eve's fate. Eve's story marks the end of the reign of the Queen of Heaven and the beginning of the sovereignty of the King of the Universe.

Monotheism was a revolutionary shift in consciousness—acknowledging a Supreme Being that transcends gender, animates, and encompasses all. Hiding the feminine aspect of the Divine and glorifying only the masculine distorts the fundamental theology of monotheism. In an effort to wipe out pagan ways, the Divine Feminine was suppressed. Yet her flame has never died.

The Bible has two versions of the creation of woman. The break between the two versions marks the break between old ways of worshipping deity of both genders and the emergence of monotheistic patriarchy, a tension that runs throughout the Bible. In chapter one of Genesis, woman was created simultaneously and equally with man as the feminine half of an androgynous primordial human created in the image of the Creator, male and female. In Hebrew, "Adam" was a generic term for human being and does not suggest maleness, so the traditional translation of "man" is misleading. In Genesis chapter two's version, the Creator shaped a creature from water and dust, breathed life into it and instructed, "From the Tree of Knowing Good and Evil you shall not eat." In the very next line the Creator stated, "It is not good for the human to be alone" and from Adam's side made woman. *Tsela*, usually translated as "rib," also means "side." Eve was formed from the feminine side of the primordial human. The human was now divided into two complementary beings.

As we seek out the matriarchal truth embedded in the Bible, we question why Eve listened to the snake and ate from the forbidden tree. In Goddess worship, the serpent was a wisdom figure and symbol for the creative energy that animates us. To ancient Hebrews, the forbidden tree of Eden was understood to represent the sacred sycamore fig associated with the Queen of Heaven—the Goddess of Canaan. Because Eve listened to the snake and ate the fruit of the forbidden tree, the male deity put "enmity" between women and the snake and all that the snake represented: "I will put enmity between you and the woman, and between your offspring and hers." (Genesis 3:15) Eve's story warned the Hebrews to reject the worship of female deity and its accompanying matriarchal customs and sexual freedom for women. The underlying message was, listen to Her voice and you will be punished!

Eve has been unfairly blamed as a temptress, responsible for the fall of man. But Eve did not act alone. Notice that Adam was right beside her while she ate the fruit of the forbidden tree. He said nothing. She shared the fruit with him. He ate. Both realized that they were "naked" after they ate of the fruit of the tree of knowledge. Yet because Eve ate the fruit first, she is identified as a sexual temptress. What is the connection between defying authority in a quest for knowledge and the act of sexual seduction? The forbidden fruit was a metaphor for the rituals of sacred sexuality connected with Goddess worship. In the patriarchal religions with roots in the Bible—Judaism, Christianity, and Islam—women's sexuality was suspect and became a matter for male ownership and control. Christianity considered Eve "the root of all evil," and blamed her for original sin. Rabbi Joseph Telushkin explains: "In Christian theology, eating the forbidden fruit constitutes the Original Sin that taints all future human beings with a primal transgression. Such sinfulness can supposedly be overcome through baptism and acceptance of the divinity of Jesus Christ who died to atone for humankind's sins. The prevailing

George Frederick Watts, *She Shall Be Called Woman*

attitude among Jewish scholars is that people sin *as* Adam and Eve sinned, not *because* they sinned." [1]

Was all that transpired in Eden a setup by the Creator? The Holy One had set forth just one rule for Eve and Adam: "You may eat freely of all the trees in the garden. But you must not eat from the Tree of Knowing Good and Evil." (Genesis 2:16,17) Did the Creator's infinite knowledge include reverse psychology? Rebellion against our creators and protectors is planted deeply in the human psyche. As we mature, we question and test our parents until it is

time to leave their gardens. Then we become obsessed with finding a mirror half who feels like "bone of my bones, and flesh of my flesh." (Genesis 2:23) Most humans leave childhood and their parents' homes to live as couples, to create and procreate. We live out our days, until we return to dust, in alternating cycles of exile-disconnection and paradise-connection with our mates, our souls, and the Divine. Perhaps Eve and Adam were ready to defy the parental rule-making deity and begin to create their independent life together. Maybe Elohim was ready, too.

Eve's rebellion was our first biblical clue that the Creator gave humans free will. Eve faced a conundrum in the garden: Safety through passive acceptance, or knowledge through independence and risk? Risking immediate death, Eve tested the truth of the edict, "You must not eat from the Tree of Knowing Good and Evil; for the day you eat from it you shall die!" (Genesis 2:17) Instead of dying, Eve (Life-Giver) became the "Mother-of-All-Who-Live," a title she shares with virtually every goddess of the ancient Near East. Eve was the first human to embody the divine process of creation.

Eve was created in the image of the Female Divine presence. Kabbalah, the Jewish mystical tradition that means "to receive," honors the Female Divine presence and calls her Shekhina, the higher power that dwells within. We feel her presence when lighting candles and when making love. She is Mother Nature. Rabbi Shoni Lebowitz says: "Shekhina, the Hebrew Goddess, has wings that transport your soul from one state of consciousness to another." Shekhina opens the curtain so we may glimpse the Infinite One.

Eve was created in the image of the Shekhina—an oft-hidden yet inextinguishable presence within the stories of all the biblical mothers. As we honor Eve for her courage, her search for knowledge, and her creative spirit, we also honor the Feminine Divine—in the ancient days and in the present, in Eve and in ourselves. ◉◉

Thomas Cole, *Expulsion from the Garden of Eden*

SARAH
"Chieftainess"
Sahrah

GENESIS : CHAPTER 11

29 Sarai was the name of Abram's wife . . . 30 Sarai was barren, she had no child.

31 Terah took his son Abram, his grandson Lot, and his daughter-in-law Sarai from Ur of the Chaldeans to go to the land of Canaan. But when they had come as far as Haran, they settled there.

GENESIS : CHAPTER 12

Yah said to Abram:
"Go forth, from your country, your people and your parent's house, to the land that I will show you. 2 I will make you a great nation and I will bless you. I will make your name great, and you will be a blessing. 3 I will bless those who bless you; and curse those who curse you; all peoples on earth will bless themselves through you."

5 Abram left with Sarai and Lot. They took all their property and the kindred souls who had joined them in Haran. They set out for the land of Canaan and they arrived there. 6 Abram journeyed through the land as far as Shechem, by the Oak of Moreh. The Canaanite was then in the land. 7 Yah appeared to Abram and said, "Unto thy seed will I give this land." So Abram built an altar there to Yah—who had appeared to him. 8 Then they moved on.

10 And there was a famine in the land so they went down to Egypt to stay for a while, for the famine was grievous in the land. 11 As they were about to enter Egypt, Abram said to Sarai, "Look, I know what a beautiful woman you are. 12 When the Egyptians see you, they will say, 'She's his wife.' And they will kill me but let you live. 13 So please tell them you are my sister so they will treat me well and spare my life because of you."

14 When they arrived in Egypt the Egyptians indeed did see that Sarai was very beautiful. 15 Pharaoh's officers saw her, praised her highly to Pharaoh, and she was taken into Pharaoh's palace. 16 Abram was well treated because of her. He was given sheep, cattle, donkeys, camels and slaves. 17 But Yah inflicted Pharaoh's household with serious plagues of disease on account of Sarai.

18 Pharaoh summoned Abram, "Why have you done this to me?" he said. "Why did you not tell me this is your wife? 19 Why did you say, 'She is my sister,' so that I took her for my wife? Now here she is. Take her and go!" 20 Pharaoh gave his people orders to send Abram and Sarai on their way.

James Tissot, *Abram's Counsel to Sarai* (detail)

Some time later, the word of Yah came to Abram
in a vision:
"Do not be afraid, Abram
I am your shield
Thy reward shall be very great."

2 Abram answered, "Yah Elohim, what can you
give me since I am childless? 3 Since you have
granted me no offspring, the man in charge of my
household, Eliezer from Damascus, will be my
heir."

4 The word of Yah came to him in reply, "That one
shall not be your heir; one who shall come from
your own body will be your heir." 5 The Infinite
One took him outside and said, "Look up at the
heavens and count the stars if you can. So shall your
descendants be."

GENESIS : CHAPTER 16

Sarai had no children with Abram, but she had an
Egyptian handmaiden named Hagar.

2 So Sarai said to Abram, "Since Yah has kept me
from having children, go into my handmaiden.
Perhaps I shall have children through her." Abram
listened to Sarai's voice. 3 After they had dwelt
in Canaan for ten years, Sarai took Hagar, her
Egyptian maid, and gave her to her husband Abram
as his wife.

4 He slept with Hagar and she became pregnant.
When she knew she had conceived, she began to
look down upon her mistress. 5 Sarai told Abram,
"This is your fault! I put my maidservant in your
arms and now that she's pregnant she looks with
contempt at me."

Follower of Matthias Stommer, *Sarah Presenting Hagar to Abraham*

6 Abram replied, "Your maid is in your hands, treat
her as you please!"

Sarai treated her so harshly that Hagar ran away.
7 The angel of Yah found Hagar by a spring in the
desert and 8 asked, "Hagar, maid of Sarai, where
have you come from, and where are you going?"

"I am escaping from my mistress Sarai," she
answered.

9 The angel of Yah told her,
"Return to your mistress and submit to her.
10 I will make your descendants too numerous
to be counted. 11 Behold, you are now with child
and will bear a son whom you shall name Ishmael
(Yah Hears), for I have heard your suffering.

12 A wild donkey of a man he'll be.
His hand will be against every man, and every
man's hand against him.
He will live at odds with all his kin."

13 Hagar called Yah, who had spoken directly to
her, El Roi. For she said, "I have now seen the One
who watches over me." 14 This is why the well is
called the Well of the Living-One-Who-Sees-Me.

15 And Hagar gave birth to a son. Abram gave
his son by Hagar the name Ishmael. 16 Abram was
eighty-six years old when Hagar bore Ishmael.

GENESIS : CHAPTER 17

When Sarai was eighty-nine years old and her
husband Abram was ninety-nine years old, Yah
appeared to him and said, "I am El-Shaddai.
Live in my presence and be blameless. 2 I will
make a covenant between us and will make you
exceedingly numerous." 3 Abram bowed with
his face to the ground.

Elohim spoke with Abram, saying,

4 "This is my covenant with you. You will become
the father of a multitude of nations. And you will
5 no longer be called Abram (Exalted Father); your
name shall be Abraham (Father of a Multitude),
6 for I will make you exceedingly fertile, and I
will make many nations come from you, and rulers
come from you. 7 I will maintain my covenant
between myself and you, and your descendants
after you, generation after generation, as a covenant
in perpetuity, to be your Elohim and the Elohim of
your descendants after you. 8 And to you and your
descendants, I shall give the country where you are
now dwelling, the entire land of Canaan, to own
in perpetuity."

9 And Elohim told Abraham,
"For your part, you and all your descendants,
for all generations, will keep my covenant.
10 This is how you and all your descendants after
you will keep my covenant: every male among
you must be circumcised. 11 You must cut the flesh
of your foreskin, and that will be the sign of the
covenant between me and you. 12 Throughout the
generations, at the age of eight days, every male
child must be circumcised. . . . 13 Thus my covenant
will be marked in your flesh as an everlasting pact."

15 Then Elohim told Abraham,
"Sarai shall no longer be called Sarai (Princess) but
Sarah (Chieftainess). 16 I will bless her and give her
a son. I will bless her so that she will be the mother
of nations, and rulers will issue from her."

17 Abraham flung himself on his face laughing, and
said to himself, "Is a child to be born to a man who
is one hundred years old? Will Sarah give birth at
ninety years old?"

18 Abraham said to Elohim, "May you acknowledge
Ishmael."

19 Elohim replied, "Your wife Sarah will bear a
son, and you will call him Isaac. I shall maintain
my covenant with him, an everlasting covenant with
all his descendants. 20 As for Ishmael, I heard you;
I will bless him and will make him fruitful and
numerous. He will be father of twelve chieftains
and I will make him into a great nation. 21 But
my covenant I shall establish with Isaac whom
Sarah will give birth to at this time next year."

22 The Infinite One finished speaking to Abraham
and ascended.

GENESIS : CHAPTER 18

Yah appeared at the Oak of Moreh, while Abraham sat at the tent entrance in the heat of the day. 2 Abraham looked up and saw three beings standing nearby. As soon as he saw them, he ran from the entrance of the tent to greet them, bowed to the ground 3 and said,

"My lords, if I find favor in your eyes, do not pass me by. 4 Let me bring a little water for you to wash your feet. Have a rest under the tree's shade.
5 Let me get you something to eat so that you can be refreshed before going further."

"Very well," they answered. "Do as you say."

6 So Abraham hurried into the tent to Sarah. "Quick," he said, "knead some of the best flour and bake some cakes." 7 Then running to the herd, Abraham took a fine and tender calf and gave it to a servant, who hurried to prepare it. 8 Then he brought some curds and milk and the calf that had been prepared, and set these before them. While they ate, he stood by them under the tree.

9 "Where is Sarah?" they asked him. And Abraham said, "Behold, in the tent."

Then the Infinite One said, 10 "I will appear to you again this time next year, and Sarah will have a son."

Sarah was listening by the tent-opening behind them. 11 Now Sarah was very old, she had stopped having her monthly periods long ago, 12 so she laughed to herself thinking, "Now that I'm past menopause, am I to be moist with pleasure, and when my husband is so old?"

13 Yah asked Abraham, "Why did Sarah laugh and think she is too old to have a child? 14 Is anything too wondrous for Yah? In the time life ripens I will return to you, and Sarah will have a son."

15 Sarah denied it, saying, "I didn't laugh," because she was frightened.

But Yah said, "Yes, you did laugh."

GENESIS : CHAPTER 20

Sarah and Abraham traveled on to the Negev and settled there for awhile. While they were staying in Gerar, 2 they told people that they were sister and brother. The king of Gerar, Abimelech, sent for Sarah and took her.

3 One night, Elohim visited Abimelech in a dream, and said, "You are a dead man, because the woman you have taken is a married woman."

4 But Abimelech had not come into her, so he said, "Would you kill someone who is innocent? 5 Didn't the man tell me, 'She is my sister'? And didn't she also say, 'He is my brother'? I did this with integrity in my heart and in innocence."

6 Elohim said to him in a dream, "I know that you did this with integrity in your heart. I, too, prevented you from sinning against me, that is why I held you back from touching her. 7 Now send them back, for they are prophets, and they will pray for you and you will live. But if you do not return her, you should know that it means death to you and all yours."

Adrien van der Werfft, *Expulsion of Hagar* (detail)

8 Early the next morning, Abimelech summoned his court and told them the whole story. They were very frightened. 9 Then Abimelech called Abraham in and asked him, "What have you done to us? What wrong have I done you, for you to bring such guilt on me and on my kingdom? You had no right to treat me like this! 10 What possessed you to do such a thing?"

11 Abraham told the king: "I thought that there was no awe of Elohim in this place and that I would be killed because of my wife. 12 In truth, she really is my sister, my father's daughter though not my mother's, and she became my wife. 13 When Elohim made me wander far from my father's house, I asked Sarah, 'Do me the kindness of telling people, every place we shall go, "He is my brother."'"

14 Abimelech gave sheep, cattle and slaves to Abraham and returned Sarah to him. 15 Abimelech told them, "Dwell anywhere in this land that pleases you." 16 He told Sarah, "I am giving your brother a thousand silver shekels so that everyone will see that you are not to blame." 17 Then Yah healed Abimelech and his wife and female slaves so that they could have children, 18 for Yah had closed up all the wombs of the women of the household because of Sarah.

Now Yah visited Sarah and did what had been promised. 2 Sarah conceived and gave birth to a son, at the time Elohim had said she would. 3 Abraham named his newborn son, the son whom Sarah had given birth to, Isaac (He Laughs). 6 For Sarah said, "Elohim has played a joke on me. All who hear about this will laugh! 7 Who would have said that Sarah would nurse children? Yet I have given birth to a son in my old age."

8 The child grew; and a great feast was given on the day Isaac was weaned. 9 Sarah saw the son of Hagar the Egyptian playing. 10 So Sarah told Abraham to drive out the maid and her son so that Ishmael would not share Isaac's inheritance. 11 Abraham was greatly distressed by this because he cared about his son. 12 But Elohim said to Abraham, "Do not distress yourself because of Ishmael and Hagar. Whatever Sarah tells you, listen to her voice. Isaac is the one through whom your name will live. 13 As for the son of Hagar, I will make him a great nation too."

14 Early the next morning, Abraham took some bread and a skin of water, and giving them to Hagar, put them on her shoulder and sent her away with the child. She wandered off into the desert of Beersheba. 15 When the skin of water was finished, she abandoned the child under a bush, 16 then she went and sat about a bowshot away, thinking, "I cannot watch my child dying." Sitting at a distance, she burst into tears.

17 Elohim heard the crying, and an angel of Elohim called to Hagar from heaven, saying, "What is wrong, Hagar? Do not be afraid, for Elohim has heard the boy's cry. 18 Lift him up and hold him in your arms, for I will make a great nation of him."

19 Then Elohim opened Hagar's eyes and she saw a well, so she went and filled the skin with water and gave the boy a drink. 20 Elohim was with the boy, and he grew up and became an archer. 21 He lived in the wilderness of Paran, and his mother found him a wife from the land of Egypt.

sarah

Some time later, Elohim tested Abraham. Elohim called, "Abraham."

"Here I am," he said. 2 The Infinite One said, "Take your son, your only one, the one you love, take Isaac, and go to the land of Moriah. Offer him as a burnt offering on one of the mountains I will show to you."

3 Early the next morning Abraham saddled his donkey and took two young men and Isaac his son with him. He chopped wood for the burnt offering and set out for the place Elohim had told him about. 4 On the third day, Abraham looked up and saw the place in the distance. 5 Then Abraham said to the men, "Stay here with the donkey. The boy and I will go up there. We will worship and will return to you."

6 Abraham took the wood for the burnt offering and loaded it on Isaac his son. He took the firestone and the knife in his hand. Then the two of them set out together. 7 Isaac spoke to Abraham his father, "Father, here are the firestone and the wood, but where is the lamb for the burnt offering?" 8 Abraham answered, "My son, Elohim will provide the lamb for the burnt offering." And the two of them went on together.

Charles-Paul Landon, *Hagar Giving Ishmael Water from the Miraculous Well in the Desert*

9 When they arrived at the place that Elohim indicated to him, Abraham built an altar there and arranged the wood. He bound his son and put him on the altar on top of the wood.

10 Then Abraham reached for the knife to slaughter his son.

11 But the angel of Yah called to him from heaven saying, "Abraham, Abraham!"

Abraham replied, "Here I am."

12 "Do not raise your hand against the boy," the angel said. "Do not harm him, for I know now that you fear Elohim. You have not refused me your son, your only one."

13 When Abraham looked up, his eye fell on a ram caught in the thicket by its horns. Abraham took the ram and offered it as a burnt offering in place of his son.

15 The angel of Yah called Abraham again from heaven. 16 "I swear because you have done this, because you have not refused me your beloved son, 17 I will shower blessings on you and make your descendants numerous as the stars of heaven and the grains of sand on the seashore."

19 Abraham then returned to his young men, and they departed together for Beersheba. And Abraham settled in Beersheba.

GENESIS : CHAPTER 23

Sarah lived for a hundred and twenty-seven years. 2 When Sarah died at Kiriat Arba, now Hebron, in the land of Canaan, Abraham stayed by her side, mourning her and weeping for her. 3 Then he arose from beside his dead wife and spoke to the sons of Het. 4 "I am a stranger and soujourner among

you. Give me a burial place, so that I may bury my Sarah."

5 The sons of Het told Abraham, 6 "You are exalted by Elohim. Take the choicest of our burial places. There is not one among us who would deny her a grave."

7 Abraham bowed low before the people of the land. 8 And he said to them, "If you find it in your soul to bury my dead, please listen and intercede for me with Ephron. 9 Let him sell me the cave of Machpelah, at the edge of his fields. Let him sell it to me, in your presence, at full market price, to use as the burial site in your midst."

10 Ephron the Hittite replied to Abraham in the presence of the children of Het, 11 "No, listen to me; I give you the land and the cave that is on it. I give it to you in the presence of my people. Bury your dead."

12 Again Abraham bowed low before the people of the land. 13 He spoke to Ephron in the presence of the people of the land, saying "Listen to me, I will pay the price of the land. Accept it from me that I may bury my dead there."

14 Ephron answered Abraham, 15 "My lord, listen to me, the land is worth four hundred shekels of silver — what is that between you and me? Bury your dead."

16 Abraham heard Ephron and weighed out for him the four hundred shekels of silver that had been discussed in the presence of the sons of Het.

19 After this, Abraham buried Sarah in the cave of the field of Machpelah, facing Mamre, which is now Hebron, in the land of Canaan.

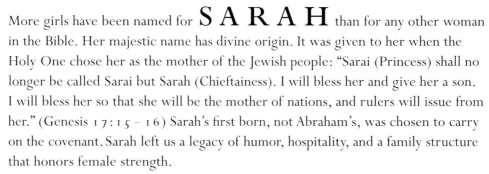

More girls have been named for S A R A H than for any other woman
in the Bible. Her majestic name has divine origin. It was given to her when the
Holy One chose her as the mother of the Jewish people: "Sarai (Princess) shall no
longer be called Sarai but Sarah (Chieftainess). I will bless her and give her a son.
I will bless her so that she will be the mother of nations, and rulers will issue from
her." (Genesis 17:15 – 16) Sarah's first born, not Abraham's, was chosen to carry
on the covenant. Sarah left us a legacy of humor, hospitality, and a family structure
that honors female strength.

       The name Sarah comes from the Hebrew root word meaning
"to command." Throughout her life, Sarah acted with the confident authority of
a high priestess; much about her life, in fact, suggests that Sarah *was* a priestess.
In the twenty-first century B.C.E., when Sarah came into womanhood, the rituals
of the Goddess religion were at their height. Ur and Haran—where she lived
before going to Canaan—were centers of moon veneration and Goddess worship.
Royalty and ritual leadership were inextricably connected in the pagan societies
of the ancient Near East. Since Sarai was a princess, it is highly likely that she was
also a priestess of the Goddess before being divinely selected as the mother of the
Jewish people.[3]

       Priestesses were powerful spiritual women who commanded
authority over the members of their households. High priestesses married
but remained childless, as did Sarah; they drank a special potion to keep sterile
and thin. If a high priestess wanted a child, she could assign another woman to
her husband for childbearing, as Sarah did with Hagar.

Priestesses engaged in rituals of sacred sexuality. The high priestess, representing the all-powerful Moon Goddess, deity of female fertility, would perform the seasonal ritual of *hieros gamos* (sacred marriage) with kings who represented gods. This holy ceremony was believed to bring fertility back to the land. Sarah may have been welcomed into the harems of the Pharaoh and the King of Gerar to participate in sacred marriage.

Sarah and Abraham must have been extraordinarily close: wife and husband, sister and brother. Although Sarah and Abraham had the same father, their relationship wasn't considered incestuous because kinship was traced exclusively through the mother in the societies of Ur and Haran. Siblings with different mothers could marry and often did in the ruling clans. As Abraham explained to the King of Gerar, "In truth she really is my sister, my father's daughter though not my mother's, and she became my wife." (Genesis 20:12)

They were a team, a partnership of equals. Legend says that Sarah was the spiritual guide and leader of the women, while Abraham led the men. Sarah was known for her generous hospitality, an attribute of Jewish womanhood that has been passed on through the generations. According to the midrash, the four sides of Sarah's tent were kept open so that all could see her hearth fire burning, its warmth welcoming travelers from every direction. A numinous cloud of glory hovered above the entrance of the tent. Her Sabbath candles cast eternal light within.[4]

Sarah controlled her household but she did not always control her feelings. She laughed at angels. Sarah saw humor in Yah's promise that she would have a child at age ninety, then lied about having laughed when confronted. Sarah's laughter expressed a range of emotions from skepticism and embarrassment to pure joy. When her son Isaac was born, she said, "Elohim has played a joke on me. All who hear about this will laugh! . . . Yet I have given birth to a son." (Genesis 21:6,7) Her laughter at this time could be interpreted as either unbridled delight or fear of ridicule. The name Isaac comes from the Hebrew root word for "laugh," and laughter remains an essential part of Sarah's legacy to us. She is the mother of Jewish humor.

Abel Pann
Genesis 18:12, "She laughed to herself" (detail)

We celebrate Sarah's luminosity and laughter, but we struggle with her darker side. Can we accept Sarah's jealous rage toward Hagar? Certainly anyone who has ever felt the agony of jealousy can relate to Sarah. She would have chosen the most physically appealing, intelligent woman in her household as the surrogate mother for her child. Imagine your mate, of eighty monogamous years, in bed with a much younger, very beautiful woman. Imagine that when the woman becomes pregnant with your husband's child, she lets you know that she loves your husband and despises you. Sarah's jealousy was understood by Elohim, who supported her decision to remove Hagar and her son, Ishmael, from her sight and told Abraham, "Do not distress yourself because of Ishmael and Hagar. Whatever Sarah tells you, listen to her voice." (Genesis 21:12)

Sarah could not control the plan Yah had for her. Her genes were meant to imprint the Hebrew tribes. The Egyptian handmaiden Hagar would be foremother to the Arab peoples. At the great feast in celebration of weaning Isaac, "Sarah saw the son of Hagar the Egyptian playing." (Genesis 21:9) The word "playing" to describe Ishmael's actions held the same triple entendre in ancient Hebrew as they do in modern English. Was Ishmael simply having fun, or mocking, or acting out sexually? Was Sarah protecting her son or her territory? Did Sarah, the prophetess, see that there would always be animosity between her descendants and those of Hagar? Or did Sarah, the jealous woman, create the breach?

Sarah's life was blessed, but far from easy. After a lifetime without children, Sarah bore a son at age ninety. How horrifying it must have been to hear that Abraham had tied up their son and taken a knife to sacrifice him. Legend tells that when Satan, in the form of an old, meek, and humble man, told Sarah about the binding of Isaac, her soul flew from her body, and she died of shock.

Sarah, the mother of Judaism, foreshadowed Mary, the mother of Christianity. They both conceived miraculously, then had Yah ask for their sons as blood sacrifice. Both sons carried the wood for their own sacrifice on their backs.

The Bible leaves us with some mystery about the twilight of Sarah's days, following the binding of Isaac. All we're told is that she lived for one hundred and twenty-seven years. She's the only woman in the Bible whose life span is given. Sarah was buried in the cave of Machpelah in Hebron—to this day the site of enmity and bloodshed between the descendants of Sarah and Hagar. Yet the positive influence of Sarah also remains with us. The central rituals of Jewish women's spiritual practice harken back to the ancient days of Sarah, our first matriarch, when rituals that honored the Feminine Divine were brought, by Sarah, into worship of the Holy One. Rabbi Lynn Gottlieb, in her book, *She Who Dwells Within,* tells us that baking bread on holy days was an ancient custom in Goddess worship. Braiding the challah comes from braiding bread to resemble the hair of Berches, the goddess of the hearth. The word *sabbath* comes from *shabbatu,* a monthly ritual celebrating the complete rest of the Moon Goddess during her menses. The midrash says that long before the Torah was given, Sarah lit candles. One of the most important functions of the high priestess of the Moon Goddess was tending the sacred flame. This flame, representing the fertilizing energy of the moonlight, was never allowed to die.[5] The daughters of Sarah guard the flame still. As we kindle Sabbath candles, as we bake and braid holy-day bread, we are connecting with Sarah and honoring the aspect of the Feminine Divine in the Holy One. ❧

REBECCA
"Tether"
Rivkah

GENESIS : CHAPTER 24

By now Abraham was a very old man, blessed by Yah in every way. 2 Abraham called for his servant, the elder of his household, who was in charge of all he had. "Pray put your hand under my thigh," Abraham requested. 3 "I want you to swear by Yah, the Elohim of Heaven and the Elohim of Earth, that you will not choose a wife for my son from the daughters of the Canaanites among whom I have settled. 4 Go to the land of my birth, and take a wife for Isaac."

5 The servant responded, "What if the woman is not willing to come back to this land? Shall I then take your son back to the country you came from?"

6 "Beware that you do not bring my son back there," Abraham answered. 7 "Yah, Elohim of Heaven, who took me from my father's house and from the country where I was born, who spoke to me and who swore to me, saying, 'I will give this land to your seed,' will send an angel ahead of you, so that you can find a wife from there, for my son. 8 If the woman is unwilling to follow, you will be released from this vow. No matter what, you are not to bring my son back to the country from which I came."

9 The servant placed his hand under Abraham's thigh, and swore. 10 Then the senior servant, head of all under the roof of Abraham, took ten camels and loaded them with precious gifts and set out to journey to Aram-Naharaim, the land of two rivers, to the city of Nahor. 11 Toward evening, at the time the women came to draw water, the servant had the camels kneel down by the well outside of town. 12 Then he said, "Yah, Elohim of my master Abraham, give me success today. Show tenderness for Abraham. 13 While I stand by the well, as the women of the town go to draw water, 14 may a girl come who I will ask to lower her jug so that I may drink. Let her say, 'Drink and let me water your camels also.' Let her be the one unveiled for Isaac. Through her may I see the tenderness you show to my lord."

15 Before he had even finished praying from his heart, Rebecca appeared with a jug on her shoulder. 16 The girl was exceedingly beautiful, virginal, untouched. She went down to the spring, filled her jug and came up.

Thomas Rossiter, *Rebecca at the Well*

Arthur Reginald, *Rebecca*

17 He ran to her, asking for a sip of water from her jar. 18 "Drink," she said, and lowered her jug to let him drink. 19 When he had enough, she said, "I shall draw water for your camels too, until they drink their fill." 20 She quickly emptied her pitcher into the trough, and ran again to the well and drew for all his camels. 21 The man was amazed at her. He was speechless. Had Yah made his journey successful?

22 As the camels finished drinking, the man took a golden nose ring and two heavy gold bracelets and asked, 23 "Whose daughter are you? Please tell me. Is there room at your father's house for us to spend the night?"

24 She answered, "I am Bethuel's daughter. Milcah and Nahor are my grandmother and grandfather. 25 Yes, there is straw, and yes, there is more than enough feed. Also there is room for you to spend the night."

26 The servant bowed low before Yah and said, 27 "Bless Yah who has not held back tenderness nor hidden his trust from my Abraham. Yah has led me on a journey to the house of Sarah and Abraham's relatives."

28 The maiden ran to her mother's house to tell what had happened. 29 Now Rebecca had a brother named Laban who hurried out to the man at the well. 30 As soon as he had seen the nose ring and the bracelets his sister was wearing, and heard Rebecca's story, he went to the man who was standing by his camels near the spring. 31 He said, "Come in, you who are blessed by Yah. Why are you standing outside? I have already made room in the house and cleared a place for the camels."

32 So the man went to the house, and the camels were unburdened. Straw and fodder were brought for the camels, and water for him and his men to wash their feet. 33 Then food was set before him, but he insisted that he could eat nothing until he told them why he had come. "Speak out," they responded.

34 "A servant of Abraham am I," he began. 35 "Yah has blessed my master, enriched him, given him sheep and cattle, silver and gold, servants and maids, camels and donkeys. 36 My lord's wife, Sarah, gave birth to a son in her old age and made him heir to all they had. 37 Abraham made me vow not to take a wife for their son from the Canaanite daughters in whose country we live. 38 He sent me here to the land of their father, to their own kin, to bring back a wife for their son.

39 "I said to my master, 'Suppose that the girl will not agree to go with me?' and 40 he said to me, 'Yah, who has walked beside me, will place an angel before you. Your way will be smoothed, you will find our son a wife among family, from within our clan. 41 You will be free from your responsibility only if you approach my kin and they refuse you.'

42 "Today, I came to the spring and prayed, 'Yah, Elohim of my master Abraham, if you are smoothing the way I walk, please grant me success in the journey I have made. 43 See, I am standing beside a well of water. If a young woman comes out to draw water and I say to her, 'Please give me a little water to drink from your jug,' 44 and if she says, 'Drink and I will draw water for your camels also,' let her be the woman that Yah has chosen for Isaac.

45 "Before I finished praying in my heart, Rebecca came out, with her jug on her shoulder. She went down to the spring and drew water, and I asked her to please give me a drink. 46 She quickly lowered the jar on her shoulder and said, 'Drink and I will water your camels also.' . . .

49 "So now if you are going to deal kindly and truly to my master, tell me; and if not let me know." 50 Laban and Bethuel replied, "This has unfolded from Yah," they said. "It is not for us to say if it is good or bad. 51 Rebecca is there before you, bring her to your lord's son, as Yah has directed."

52 As he heard their words, Abraham's servant prostrated himself before Yah. 53 Then he brought out silver and gold ornaments and clothes which he gave to Rebecca. He also gave precious objects to her mother and brother. 54 They ate and drank, he and his companions, and spent the night there. When they got up the next morning, he said, "Let me go back to my master now." 55 Rebecca's mother and brother said, "Let the girl stay with us for ten days or so; then she can go." 56 But the servant replied, "Don't hold me back, since Yah has made my journey successful; let me leave and go to my master."

57 They said, "Let us call the girl and hear the answer from her own lips." 58 Calling Rebecca, they asked her, "Will you go with this man?"

"I will go!" she told them.

59 So they let Rebecca go, with her nurse, and Abraham's servant and his men.

60 They blessed Rebecca and said to her:
"Our sister, may you mother thousands and tens of thousands.
May your seed inherit the gate of those who hate them."
61 Rebecca rose, with her young women, mounted the camels and followed the man. And they departed.

62 Isaac had come back from the Well-of-the-Living-One-Who-Sees-Me and was settled in the Negev desert. 63 He was out in the field meditating at sunset. When he opened his eyes, look, there were the camels approaching. 64 Rebecca also looked up and saw Isaac. She fell from the camel 65 and asked, "Who is that man in the field walking towards us?"

"That is my lord," said the servant, so she reached for her veil and covered herself.

66 The servant told Isaac the whole story. 67 Then Isaac brought her into his mother Sarah's tent, and Rebecca became his wife. And in his love for her he found comfort after his mother's death.

GENESIS : CHAPTER 25

20 Isaac was forty years old when Rebecca came to him. 21 And he prayed to Yah on Rebecca's behalf, for she was barren. Yah heard his prayer and Rebecca conceived. 22 But the children so clashed inside her that she said, "If this be so, then why do I exist?"

She went to question Yah.

23 And Yah said to her,
"There are two nations in your womb,
two separate peoples shall come from your body.
One will be mightier than the other,
and the elder will serve the younger."

24 When the time came for her to give birth, there were twins in her womb. 25 The first to come out was ruddy, with hair all over him, like a coat; so they named him Esau (Rough-One). 26 And then his brother came out, with his hand grasping Esau's heel, so they called him Jacob (Heel-Holder). Isaac was sixty years old when Rebecca gave birth to twins.

27 When the boys grew up, Esau became a skilled hunter, a man of the open country. Jacob was a quiet man, staying at home among the tents. 28 Isaac favored Esau because he brought him wild game to eat; but Rebecca loved Jacob.

Andrea Vaccaro, *Encounter between Rebecca and Isaac*

29 One day when Jacob was cooking a lentil stew, Esau returned from the countryside exhausted. 30 "Let me gulp down some of that red stuff, I am famished," Esau begged Jacob.

31 Jacob replied, "Sell me your birthright today."

32 Esau said, "I am dying of hunger; what good is a birthright to me?" 33 But Jacob said, "Swear to me today." So Esau swore to him and sold his brother his birthright. 34 Then Jacob gave Esau bread and lentil stew. Esau ate, drank, got up and went away. That was all Esau cared about his birthright.

GENESIS : CHAPTER 26

Once again famine gripped the land, different from the famine in the time of Sarah and Abraham. So Isaac went to Abimelech the Philistine king, in Gerar. 2 And Yah appeared to Isaac and said, "Do not go down to Egypt. Live where I tell you to. 3 Dwell in this land and I will be with you and bless you. To you and your descendants I will give all these lands and confirm the oath I promised your father Abraham. 4 I will make your seed as numerous as the stars in the heavens and give them all these lands. Through your offspring all nations on earth will be blessed; 5 because Abraham obeyed my voice and kept my commandmants and laws." 6 So Isaac stayed in Gerar.

7 When the men in the place asked him about his wife, he told them that she was his sister. He was afraid that they would kill him because Rebecca was very beautiful. 8 They had been there for some time, when the king looked out of the window and saw Isaac playing with Rebecca. 9 Abimelech called to Isaac, "It's obvious that she's your wife—how dare you say that she's your sister."

Isaac said to him, "I did it because I believed that I would be killed on account of her."

10 "What have you done to us? One of the men might easily have slept with your wife, and then you would have brought blame onto us." 11 Then the king issued this order to all his people: "Whoever harms this man or woman will be put to death."

rebecca

34 When Esau was forty years old, he married Judith and Basemath. They were Hittite women and this was a source of bitter grief to Rebecca and Isaac.

GENESIS : CHAPTER 27

When Isaac was old and his sight a dim blur, he called his elder son Esau and said, 2 "Son of mine."

"Here I am," Esau replied. "Now I have grown old and I do not know the day I'll die. 3 Gather your arrows and bow and hunt some game for me. 4 Please make me a stew the way I love it, bring it to me to eat and I shall give you my soul's blessing before I die."

5 Rebecca heard Isaac speak to Esau his son. So when Esau left to go hunting, 6 Rebecca said to her son Jacob, "Listen, I just overheard your father tell your brother Esau, 7 'Bring me wild game and cook a stew for me, and I shall eat and bless you in Yah's presence before I die.'"

8 "Now, my son, listen to my voice and do what I tell you. 9 Go to the flock and bring me two tender kids, so I can prepare a tasty stew the way your father likes it. 10 You will bring it to your father and he will eat, then he will bless you before he dies."

11 Jacob answered his mother Rebecca. "But my brother Esau is hairy and my skin is smooth. 12 What if my father touches me and realizes that I'm tricking him? Then I will bring down a curse on myself and not a blessing," said Jacob.

13 His mother said, "Let the curse be on me, my son. Just listen to my voice and go fetch me the kids." 14 So Jacob went and got them and handed them to his mother; and she cooked the tasty dish his father loved. 15 Then Rebecca took some of her older son Esau's best clothes and put them on her younger son Jacob; 16 and she covered Jacob's hands and the bare part of his neck with goat skins. 17 Then she put the savory stew along with the bread she had made into her son Jacob's hands.

18 Jacob approached his father Isaac and said, "Father."

"Here I am," Isaac said. "Who are you, my son?"

19 "I am Esau, your firstborn," Jacob said to his father. "I have done as you told me. Now sit up and eat some of the game I have brought you and give me your soul's blessing."

20 And Isaac said, "How did you succeed so quickly, my son?"

"Because Yah, your Elohim, put it into my hands," Jacob replied.

21 Isaac told Jacob, "Come closer that I may feel you, my son, to know if you are my son Esau or not." 22 So Jacob came close and Isaac felt him, "The voice is Jacob's voice, yet the hands are the hands of Esau." 23 He did not recognize him because his hands were hairy like those of his brother Esau. So he blessed him. 24 Yet he asked, "Are you really my son Esau?"

"I am," said Jacob. 25 And Isaac said, "Bring me the stew so that I can eat my son's game and give you my soul's blessing." Jacob served the stew and Isaac ate; then he brought him wine and Isaac drank.

26 Then his father Isaac said to Jacob, "Come closer son, and kiss me." 27 Jacob went closer and kissed his father who sniffed the scent of his clothes. Then Isaac blessed him and said,

"Ah, the smell of my son
is like a summer field
blessed by Yah.

28 May Elohim grant you the dew of the heavens,
the richness of the earth, and
abundance of grain and wine.

29 May people serve you,
and nations bow low before you.

May you rule over your brother,
and let your mother's sons bow before you.

Cursed be those who curse you,
and blessed be those who bless you."

30 No sooner had Isaac finished the blessing and Jacob left his father, than Esau came back from hunting. 31 He, too, cooked a stew and brought it to his father and said, "Father sit up, please eat my game and give me your soul's blessing."

32 "Who are you?"

"I am your son, your firstborn, Esau."

33 A violent trembling overcame Isaac as he spoke, "Who then was he who hunted game and served me? I ate it all before you came, I blessed him and blessed he must remain."

34 When Esau heard the words of his father, he let out a loud bitter cry and begged his father, "Bless me too, my father."

35 But Isaac answered, "Your brother came in deceit and took away your blessing."

36 Esau said, "Isn't he rightly named Jacob/Heel-Holder? He has deceived me twice, first he took my birthright and now, look, he clutches my blessing. Haven't you reserved a blessing for me?"

37 Isaac replied to Esau, "I have already made him your master. I have given him all his brothers as servants, I have given him grain and wine to sustain him. So what can I do, my son?"

38 Esau asked, "Is the one blessing all you have, father? Haven't you a blessing for me too?" And Esau wept.

39 Then Isaac answered him, saying:

"Your dwelling will be the richness of the earth
and the dew of heaven above,

40 Yet, by your sword you will live,
and your brother you will serve.
Though when you rebel,
you will tear his yoke from your neck."

41 Esau held a bitter grudge against Jacob for the blessing his father had given and said to himself, "When the days of mourning my father are over, then I will kill my brother Jacob."

42 And Rebecca was told what her older son Esau had said. So she sent for her younger son Jacob and said, "Your brother Esau is consoling himself by planning to kill you, my son. 43 So now, my son, listen to my voice, arise and flee to my brother Laban in Haran. 44 Stay with him awhile until your brother's fury cools. 45 When your brother's anger against you subsides and he forgets what you've done to him, I'll send for you to return here. Why should I lose you both in one day?"

46 Rebecca said to Isaac, "I am weary of my life because of these Hittite women. If Jacob were to marry a woman of this land, my life will not be worth living."

GENESIS : CHAPTER 28

Isaac summoned Jacob and blessed him. He instructed him, "Do not marry a daughter of Canaan. 2 Go to Padam Aram, to the home of your mother's father; and marry one of the daughters of Laban, your mother's brother." 3 And Isaac blessed Jacob: "May El Shaddai bless you and make you fertile and numerous, so that you become a community of peoples. 4 May Yah give you and your descendants the blessings of Abraham and Sarah. Someday you will possess this land where you are now living as a stranger, for Elohim promised this land to your grandfather Abraham." 5 Then Isaac sent Jacob away to Rebecca's brother in Padam Aram.

6 When Esau saw that Isaac had blessed Jacob and commanded him not to take a wife from among the Canaanite women, 7 and that Jacob had obeyed his father and gone to Rebecca's family in Padam Aram to choose a wife from there, 8 Esau realized that the daughters of Canaan were evil in the eyes of his father and mother. 9 So Esau went to Ishmael, son of Abraham and Hagar, and chose Mahalat, their daughter, to be his wife, in addition to the wives he had.

10 Jacob left Beersheba and went toward Haran. 11 He came upon a certain place and stopped there for the night, for the sun had set. Taking one of the stones of the place, he laid it under his head as a pillow, and 12 he dreamed that there was a ladder rising from the earth with its top reaching the heavens, and angels of Elohim were going up and down on it.

13 And there was Yah standing beside him and saying,

"I am Yah, Elohim of your grandfather Abraham and your grandmother Sarah. And I am Elohim of your mother Rebecca and your father Isaac. The ground you camp on belongs to you. I bestow it to your seed. 14 Like grains of dust on the ground your seed will be; you will burst out to the west and east, to north and south, and all clans on earth will be blessed through you and your seed. 15 Remember that I am beside you, to watch over you wherever you go and I will bring you back to this land, and not leave you until I have fulfilled this promise."

16 When Jacob awoke from his sleep he said, "Surely Yah is in this place and I did not know. 17 He was afraid and said, "How awesome is this place. This is none other than the house of Elohim and this is the gate of heaven." 18 And Jacob started out, early in the morning. ∾

William Blake, *Jacob's Ladder*

Legend says that after Sarah's death, the light of the Shekhina that had hovered above her tent entrance disappeared. The candles that had burned within went out. For the next three years, every time Isaac entered his mother's tent and found it dark, he sank into despondency. The time had come to find a wife to comfort the forty-year-old Isaac and secure the continuity of the clan. That woman was destined to be Rebecca.

REBECCA was a woman of decisiveness

and action. As a young girl she left home without a moment's hesitation to marry Isaac. After birthing twins, Jacob and Esau, she didn't hesitate to choose one heir between them; with firm resolve, she played the trickster to insure Jacob's place as tribal leader. Led to action by Yah, Rebecca determined the course of history.

As the search for Isaac's bride began, Abraham summoned his most trusted servant, Eliezer, and told him, "Pray, put your hand under my thigh," a euphemism for his testicles. (The word testament comes from the Latin for "testicles" and refers to this custom of oath-taking.) "I want you to swear to Yah, the Elohim of the Heavens and the Elohim of the Earth," Abraham commanded, "that you will not choose a wife for my son from the daughters of the Canaanites among whom I have settled. Go to the land of my birth, and take a wife for Isaac." (Genesis 24:2-4)

Why did Abraham insist that the servant go back to Haran? Because thousands of years ago, the culture in Haran—the homeland of all the women in the first family of Genesis—was matriarchal and matrilineal. In Haran, women were recognized as individuals with rights, they were not just considered property. Women's strength was valued and their sexuality honored as sacred. Abraham wanted Isaac's mate to have the same ideas of her worth as a woman that Sarah had.

From Rebecca's own lips came the decision to leave her family to marry Isaac. With a simple and emphatic "I will go!" Rebecca, a beautiful young girl with a gold nose ring and lots of chutzpah, went off to a strange land to her unknown husband, on one of the ten camels she had watered the day before. Watering ten camels, each time lifting a heavy jug up from the spring, was not an easy task. Camels are well known for their capacity for storing enormous amounts of water. Rebecca was both generous and vigorous. She had to be strong because she was chosen by the Divine to control the leadership of the first family of monotheism.

As she approached her destination at sunset, Rebecca saw Isaac meditating. At that same moment, he looked up and saw her caravan approaching. Rebecca went into Sarah's tent with him. Legend says that when Rebecca came, the cloud of glory reappeared above the tent. The blessed light was once again lit. Joy had returned.

rebecca

Jean-Baptiste Camille Corot, *Rebecca at the Well*

Abel Pann
Genesis 26:8, "Isaac playing with Rebecca"

Rebecca and Isaac were the only absolutely monogamous couple in Genesis. They had good chemistry, as evidenced when the King of Gerar saw "Isaac playing with Rebecca." (Genesis 26:8) They were complementary but opposite in character. Isaac was a meditator, a loving and gentle but damaged man. One midrash says his eyes were dim because when he lay bound upon the altar, about to be sacrificed by his father, the angels wept and their tears fell upon his eyes. The tears remained there, weakening his sight. Another says that at the moment Isaac was about to be sacrificed, the heavens opened and he was blinded by the light of the Shekhina. Whatever the cause, Isaac's head remained in the clouds, his insight as well as his eyesight dimmed. Rebecca had clarity of vision.

In Rebecca's pregnancy, she felt a conflict inside her that Dante, in his *Paradiso,* later described as "twins infuriated already in their mother's womb." Their fight took the fight out of her. In gut-wrenching pain and despair, she pleaded to Yah, "If this be so, then why do I exist?" Yah spoke directly to Rebecca: "There are two nations in your womb . . . the elder will serve the younger." Then Rebecca understood that her purpose was to insure Jacob's leadership.

Rebecca intervened as Isaac prepared to give his soul's blessing to his favorite son, the older twin, Esau. She insisted that Jacob "listen to her voice" and follow her instructions swiftly and exactly. She promised to accept her husband's curse if her plan did not succeed. But her plan did work. Jacob received Isaac's blessing and became the father of the Twelve Tribes of Israel. Rebecca fulfilled her purpose, but our courageous foremother carried the burden of deceiving her husband, wounding her son Esau, and sending her beloved child Jacob away, never to see him again.

In a refrain of her earlier plea, Rebecca expressed the depth of her determination that the lineage be informed by a woman from her homeland by questioning the value of her life should that not happen. She said to Isaac, "If Jacob were to marry a woman of this land, my life will not be worth living." Rebecca succeeded in sending Jacob back to Haran to find a wife among women who knew their power.

Rebecca, not Isaac, was the dynamic force in the second generation. The divine plan was revealed to her and the responsiblity for carrying it out rested on her shoulders alone. Rebecca never hesitated. Her decisiveness determined destiny. ௸

RACHEL
"Ewe"
Rahchayl

LEAH
"Wearied"
Layah

GENESIS : CHAPTER 29

Continuing his journey, Jacob came to the land of the people of the east. 2 He gazed out and saw a well and three flocks of sheep lying next to it, waiting to drink from it. A huge stone was on the mouth of the well. 3 Only when all the flocks were gathered did the shepherds roll the stone from the well's mouth, water the sheep, then lay the stone back in place.

4 Jacob asked the shepherds, "My brothers, where are you from?"

"We're from Haran," they answered.

5 He said, "Do you know Laban, the grandson of Milcah and Nahor?"

"We know him," they said.

6 "Is he well?" Jacob continued.

"He is," they replied, "and here comes his daughter Rachel with the flock."

7 "Look," Jacob said. "The sun is still high; it is not yet time for the livestock to be gathered. Water the sheep and take them back to graze."

8 "We can't until all the flocks are gathered together, then we roll the stone off the well's mouth and water the sheep."

9 He was still talking to them when Rachel approached with her father's flock, for she was a shepherdess. 10 When Jacob saw Rachel, daughter of Laban, his mother's brother, he went to the stone and rolled it off the mouth of the well, and watered her sheep.

11 Then Jacob kissed Rachel and wept. 12 He told Rachel that he was her kin, Rebecca's son, and she ran to tell her father. 13 As soon as Laban heard the news of Rebecca's son Jacob, he ran out to meet him, embraced and kissed him and brought him to his house. Jacob told Laban everything that had happened.

14 "Without doubt you are of my bone and flesh," Laban said to him. And Jacob stayed with him for one month.

15 Then Laban said to Jacob, "Just because you are my nephew, why should you work for me for nothing? Tell me what can I pay you?"

Dante Gabriel Rosetti, *Dante's Vision of Rachel and Leah*

16 Now Laban had two daughters, the older named Leah, and the younger Rachel. 17 Leah was weak-eyed, but Rachel was beautiful and shapely, 18 and Jacob fell in love with her.

His answer was, "I will serve you for seven years in return for your younger daughter Rachel."

19 Laban said, "Better I give her to you than to another man. Stay with me."

20 So Jacob worked for seven years for Rachel, but they seemed like only a few days to him because of his love for her. 21 Then Jacob said to Laban, "Give me my wife, my time is fulfilled and I want to lie with her."

22 Laban gathered all the people of the place together for a feast with wine. 23 And when evening came he took his daughter Leah and brought her to Jacob, and Jacob came in to her. 24 And Laban gave his slave Zilpah to Leah to be her handmaid.

25 When morning came, look, she was Leah! So Jacob said to Laban, "Why have you done this to me? It was for Rachel that I worked with you. Why have you deceived me?"

26 Laban replied, "It is not our custom here to marry off the younger before the elder. 27 Finish this daughter's bridal week and I will give you the younger one also, in return for another seven years work."

28 Jacob agreed. He finished the week with Leah, and then Laban gave him Rachel to be his wife. 29 Laban gave his slave Bilhah to his daughter Rachel to be her handmaid. 30 Jacob lay with Rachel also, and he loved Rachel more than Leah. He worked for Laban for another seven years.

31 Yah saw that Leah was unloved and opened her womb but Rachel remained barren.

32 Leah conceived and bore a son and named him Reuben (See-a-Son), meaning Yah has seen my misery, and she said, "Now my man will love me." 33 And she conceived again and bore a son and said, "Yah has heard I am despised and has given me this one too," and she named him Simeon (Hearing). 34 Conceiving again, she gave birth to a son and said, "This time my husband will become attached to me, for I have given him three sons." So she called him Levi (Joining). 35 Fruitful, once again, she gave birth to another son and said, "This time I will praise Yah," and named him Judah (Thank-Yah). And she ceased having children.

GENESIS : CHAPTER 30

When Rachel saw that she could not bear children, she became jealous of her sister. So she said to Jacob, "Give me children, or I shall die." 2 Jacob became angry with her and said, "Am I in place of Elohim who has denied you children?" 3 And she said, "Take my handmaid Bilhah, come in to her, so that she may give birth upon my knees, and I shall have children through her." 4 Rachel gave Jacob Bilhah as a wife. He lay with her. 5 She conceived and bore a son. 6 And Rachel said, "Elohim has done justice to me, heard my voice and given me a son." Therefore she named him Dan (Justice-Is-Done).

7 Rachel's handmaid Bilhah conceived again and bore a second son. 8 Rachel said, "My sister and I struggled mightily and I have prevailed." So she called him Naftali (My Struggle).

9 Now when Leah saw that she had stopped giving birth, she took her handmaid Zilpah and gave her to Jacob as a wife. 10 Zilpah bore a son and 11 Leah said, "What fortune!" and named him Gad (Fortune). 12 And Zilpah had a second son 13 and Leah said, "How happy I am, all the women will know of my happiness." So she named him Asher (Happiness).

14 During the time of the wheat harvest, Reuben, Leah's oldest son, found some mandrakes (love-apples) out in the fields and brought them to his mother Leah.

Rachel said to Leah, "Please give me some of your son's mandrakes."

15 Leah answered, "Isn't it enough that you have taken my husband? Now you want to take my son's mandrakes, too?"

"To be fair, you may sleep with Jacob tonight, in trade for your son's mandrakes," Rachel replied.

16 When Jacob came back from the fields that night, Leah went out to meet him and told him, "You must sleep with me, because I have hired you with my son's mandrakes." On that night, he slept with her.

17 Elohim heard Leah and she became pregnant and bore a fifth son. 18 Leah said, "Elohim has given me my reward for giving my slave-girl to my husband." So she named him Issachar (There-Is-Hire).

19 Again Leah conceived and gave birth to a sixth son by Jacob, and said, 20 "Elohim has given me a fine gift. Now my husband will prize me, for I have borne him six sons." So she named this one Zebulun (Prince).

Abel Pann
Genesis 29:17, "Leah was weak-eyed"

21 Later she gave birth to a daughter and named her Dina.

22 Then Elohim remembered Rachel and heard her. Elohim opened her womb, 23 and she conceived and gave birth to a son, and she said, "Elohim has taken away my shame."

24 And she named him Joseph (Add), and said, "Yah, add another son to me."

rachel
leah

25 Now it was once Rachel gave birth to Joseph, that Jacob said to Laban, "Release me and let me go back to my country. 26 Give me my children and wives for whom I have served you, and I will be on my way. You know how hard I have worked for you!"

GENESIS : CHAPTER 31

Jacob heard that Laban's sons were saying, "Jacob has taken everything that belonged to our father and has gained all his wealth from what was our father's." 2 And Jacob noticed that Laban's attitude toward him was not as it used to be.

3 Then Yah said to Jacob, "Return to the land of your father and your kin, and I will be with you."

4 So Jacob sent for Rachel and Leah to come to the fields, where he was with the flocks. 5 He said to them, "I see by your father's face that he does not have regard for me as he did before. But Elohim has been with me. 6 You know that I have served your father with all my strength, 7 but he has tricked me and switched my wages ten times. However, Elohim has not allowed him to harm me.... 11 The angel of Elohim called to me,

in the dream, 'Jacob!' and I answered, 'Here I am.'
12 And the angel said, I have seen what Laban has
been doing to you. 13 I am the Elohim of Beth-El,
where you anointed a pillar and made a vow to
me. Now leave this land at once and go back to
the land of your birthplace."

14 Rachel and Leah replied, "Is there any share of
our father's inheritance for us? 15 He treats us like
strangers. He sold us and has completely swallowed
up our money. 16 Surely all the wealth that Elohim
took away from our father belonged to us and our
children anyway. So do whatever Elohim has told
you to do."

17 Then Jacob put his wives and children on
camels, 18 drove all the livestock ahead of them,
with all the goods he had accumulated in Paddan
Aram, to go to his father Isaac in the land of
Canaan. 19 While Laban was away shearing his
flocks, Rachel stole her father's teraphim (idols).
20 Jacob deceived Laban by not telling him he was
running away. 21 So they fled with all they owned,
crossing the Euphrates and heading towards the
hill country of Gilead.

22 Three days later Laban heard that they had fled.
23 He took his kinsman with him and pursued
them for seven days, until he caught up with them
in the hills of Gilead. 24 But when Laban dreamed
that night, Elohim came to him and told him, "Take
heed, attempt nothing with Jacob, either good or
bad."

25 Laban overtook Jacob. . . . 26 Laban said, "What
have you done? Why have you stolen my heart
and carried my daughters off like captives of war?
27 Why did you flee in secrecy? Why didn't you tell
me, so I could send you on your way with festive

music, with tambourine and lyre? 28 You didn't
even let me kiss my daughters and grandchildren
good-bye. You've done a foolish thing. 29 I have the
power to harm you, but your Elohim came to me
last night, telling me to attempt nothing with you.
30 Very well, you had to leave because you were
longing to return home; but why did you steal my
teraphim?"

31 "I was afraid, because I thought you would take
away your daughters by force," Jacob answered.
32 "But if you find anyone who has your gods, they
shall not live. In the presence of your relatives, see
for yourself, if there is anything of yours here and
take it." Now Jacob did not know that Rachel had
stolen the teraphim.

33 Laban went into Jacob's tent, and into Leah's
tent, and into the tent of the two slavewomen, and
he found nothing. Leaving Leah's tent, he entered
Rachel's tent.

34 Rachel took the teraphim, put them inside her
camel saddle and sat on them. Laban rummaged
through everything in her tent but found nothing.
35 Rachel told her father, "Forgive me for not
rising before you, but I'm having my period."
So he searched but could not find the teraphim.

GENESIS : CHAPTER 32

Early the next morning Laban kissed his
grandchildren and his daughters and blessed
them. He left and returned home.

2 Jacob went on his way, and angels of Elohim
met him. 3 When he saw them, Jacob said, "This
is the camp of Elohim." So he named that place
Mahanaim.

Raphael, *Story of Jacob: Going to Canaan*

rachel
leah

4 Jacob sent messengers ahead to his brother Esau
. . . 5 And instructed them as follows, "Say this to
my lord Esau, 'Here is the message of your servant
Jacob: I have been staying with Laban, and have
delayed there until now. 6 I own oxen, beasts of
burden, flocks, and men and women slaves. I send
news of this to my lord in hope of winning your
favor.'"

7 The messengers returned to Jacob and told him,
"We went to your brother Esau, and he is already
on his way to meet you; there are four hundred
men with him."

8 Jacob was greatly afraid, in his distress he divided
the people with him into two camps, 9 thinking,
"If Esau comes to one camp and attacks it, the other
camp may escape."

10 Then Jacob prayed, "Oh Elohim of my
grandfather Abraham and my grandmother Sarah
and my mother Rebecca and father Isaac, Oh Yah,
who said to me, 'Return to your native land and I
will be good to you,' 11 I am unworthy of all the
lovingkindness and faithfulness that you have shown
your servant. I had only my staff when I crossed
this Jordan and now I have grown into two camps.
12 Oh save me, I pray, from the hand of Esau,
for I fear him, lest he come and smite me and the
mothers with their children. 13 But you have said,
'I shall be good to you and make your descendants
as the sand by the sea, too numerous to count." . . .

23 The same night he arose and with his two wives,
and his two womenservants, and his eleven children
crossed over the ford of the Jabbok.

24 After taking them across the stream, he sent over all his possessions. 25 And Jacob was left alone. Then a being wrestled with him until the break of dawn. 26 When the being saw that it could not prevail against him, it wrenched Jacob's hip at its socket, so that the socket of his hip was strained as he wrestled with the being. 27 Then the being said, "Let me go, for dawn is breaking." But Jacob said, "I will not let you go unless you bless me." 28 Said the other, "What is your name?" He replied, "Jacob." 29 The other said, "Your name shall no longer be Jacob, but Israel, for you have wrestled with divine and human beings and won." 30 Jacob pleaded, "Please tell me your name."

The One said, "You must not ask my name!" 31 Jacob named the place Peniel, saying "I have seen Elohim face to face and I have survived."

GENESIS: CHAPTER 33

Looking up, Jacob saw Esau coming towards him with four hundred men. So Jacob divided the children among Leah, Rachel and the two womenservants. 2 He put the servants and their children in front, with Leah and her children following. Rachel and Joseph were last. 3 Jacob bowed to the ground seven times, until he came near his brother. 4 Esau ran out to meet him and embraced him and threw his arms around his neck and kissed him. They wept.

GENESIS : CHAPTER 35

And Elohim said to Jacob, "Arise, go up to Beth-El and dwell there and make an altar there to Elohim who appeared to you when you were fleeing from your brother Esau."

2 Jacob said to his household and to all who were with him, "Put away the foreign gods you have with you. Cleanse and purify yourselves and change your garments. 3 Let us go to Beth-El, to make an altar for the Elohim who heard my distress and has been with me wherever I have gone."

4 So they gave Jacob all the foreign gods in their hands and their earrings in the shape of gods and goddesses, and Jacob buried them under the great oak by Shechem. 5 They journeyed onward. A divine terror struck the towns around them, and none pursued the clan of Jacob.

8 And Deborah, Rebecca's nurse, died and was buried below Beth-El, under the tree they named the Oak of Tears.

9 Elohim appeared to Jacob again, when he returned from Padam Aram, and blessed him and said, 10 "Your name shall no longer be Jacob, but Israel shall be your name."

16 They moved on from Beth-El. While they were still some distance from Efrat, Rachel began to give birth. She had a very hard labor. 17 It was when the birthing was at its hardest that the midwife told her, "Don't be afraid, this is going to be another son for you." 18 As she breathed her last, for she was dying, she named him: Ben-Oni (Son-of-My-Suffering). But his father called him: Benjamin (Son-of-My-Right-Hand).

19 Rachel died on the road to Efrat, now Bethlehem. 20 Jacob set up a pillar over her burial-place. The same pillar that marks Rachel's grave is there today. 🐝

rachel
leah

The rivalry between **LEAH AND RACHEL** wasn't about a birthright—the Holy One chose both to be mothers of a people. Their conflict was over the love of one man, their husband, Jacob.

The first moment that Jacob set eyes on gorgeous Rachel, he kissed her and he wept. He was enchanted by her. The smooth-skinned, expressive man held nothing back. Theirs was love at first sight, a marriage "made in heaven." In Yiddish, this is called a *beshert* relationship. When the angels join you and the union is meant to be, you may know it in the first glance. Rachel and Jacob were a magnificent pair.

"Jacob worked for seven years for Rachel, but they seemed like only a few days to him because of his love for her. Then Jacob said to Laban, 'Give me my wife, my time is fulfilled and I want to lie with her.' Laban gathered all the people of the place together for a feast with wine." (Genesis 29:20–23) And when wine flows in the Bible, a plot twist is almost inevitable. Jacob awoke to find Leah at his side: "When morning came, look, she was Leah!" (Genesis 29:25) This wedding night incites the imagination and raises many questions. How could Jacob have been fooled? Was he that drunk? Where was Rachel? Did she go along with the deception because she feared her father? Did Rachel sacrifice her own happiness out of compassion—to spare her older sister humiliation?

The father set the stage for intense jealousy and rivalry between the sisters. Rachel was destined always to share her lover. Leah was forever to know it was her sister who was Jacob's beloved.

Until Leah, all the matriarchs were described as extraordinarily beautiful, which is heartening to us who live in a society that doesn't extol Jewish-

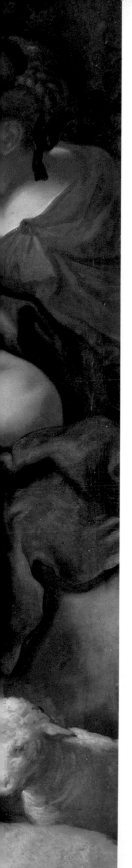

looking women as the physical ideal. But Leah's beauty was not external. The Bible says: "Leah was weak-eyed, but Rachel was beautiful and shapely." Leah represents soul connection and inner beauty.

In naming her son Judah, Leah became the first person in the Bible to express gratitude to the Infinite One. Yah hu dah means "Thank Yah!" Jewish people carry this name to this day. Leah honored the Feminine Divine by naming her second son, by her handmaid Zilpah, Asher (Happiness) after Asherah, the Mother-Goddess of the ancient Near East.

Leah was blessed with six sons and the only daughter in the family. Her husband may not have been "in love" with her, but he did make love with her often enough for her to conceive seven times. Her lineage had a formative impact on the destiny of the House of Israel: Moses, Aaron, Miriam, King David, King Solomon, Jesus of Nazareth, and most Jews alive today descend from Mother Leah.

In contrast, Rachel suffered the agony of infertility for decades. When Yah finally remembered Rachel, she bore a son, whom she named Joseph (Add), saying "Yah, add another son to me." (Genesis 30:24) In time, she got her wish, but that child cost her her life. Rachel died giving birth to Benjamin. Rachel embodied sacrifice; she was unfulfilled to the end.

One of the most telling acts of Rachel's life was her theft of her father's household idols, the *teraphim.* Were the *teraphim,* probably figurines invoking the Goddess of fertility and childbirth, sacred objects to Rachel? Or did she want to prevent her father from idol worship? In *The Hebrew Goddess,* Raphael Patai explains: "Judging from the frequent occurrence of these female figurines, not matched anywhere by images of male gods, the worship of the Goddess must have been extremely popular in all segments of Hebrew society."[6] Rachel was steadfast in her mission to hide the *teraphim,* and was punished by premature death for her actions. Her beloved cursed her unknowingly when Jacob swore to Laban that whoever had stolen his household *teraphim* "shall not live." (Genesis 31:32) Indeed, Rachel died in painful labor, birthing her second son, Benjamin. Was she punished for embracing the Divine Feminine? For thousands of years, Rachel's grave on the road to Efrat, now Bethlehem, has been a pilgrimage site for women struggling with infertility. It is said to be a place of miracles.

Johann Karl Loth, *Jacob and Rachel at the Well* (detail)

rachel
leah

Bartolomé Estaban Murillo, *Laban Searching for His Stolen Gods*

Despite her struggles, or perhaps because of them, Rachel, the stunning shepherdess, has come to be considered the soul-mother of the Jewish people. She represents redemption as well as sacrifice. Jeremiah's prophecy said that the Holy Land would be reclaimed and the people reunited because of the Divine One's compassion for Rachel. "Thus said Yah: A cry is heard in Ramah, wailing and bitter weeping; Rachel weeping for her children. She refused to be comforted for her children, who are gone. Thus Yah said: Restrain your voice from weeping, your eyes from shedding tears. For there is reward for your labor. They shall return from the enemy's land. There is hope for your future." (Jeremiah 31:15–16)

Rachel suffered, struggled, and rebelled. We come to her when we are wrestling with our own darkness, because she has been there. Rachel is the ancestress who understands, and more, she cares enough to cry for us, her children.

In Kabbalah, Rachel and Leah both are symbols of the Divine Feminine—the Shekhina. Rachel symbolizes the revealed world, while Leah symbolizes the concealed world. Rachel's domain is *Malkut,* the world of manifest energy, action, and speech. She represents divine essence taking physical form in the earthly plane. Leah's realm is *Binah,* the world of hidden energy, the dimension of mind, soul, and understanding. She represents the exalted power of deep, quiet, unseen holiness.

Rachel and Leah each embodied a different dimension of love. One aspect was passion and attraction; the other, devotion and depth. The sisters' relationship with their beloved, Jacob, is like our relationship with the Holy One. It is sustained by both passion and devotion, manifest and hidden energy. ❧

DINA
"Justice"
Deenah

GENESIS : CHAPTER 33

18 Jacob came in peace to the town of Shechem, which is in the land of Canaan, having come from Padam Aram, and he encamped facing the town. 19 He bought the parcel of land where he had pitched his tent from the sons of Hamor, father of Shechem, for one hundred pieces of silver.

GENESIS : CHAPTER 34

Now Dina, Leah's daughter by Jacob, went out to see the daughters of the land. 2 When Shechem, son of Hamor, the ruler of the land, saw her, he seized her and lay with her by force. 3 But Dina had touched his heart: he fell in love with her and spoke tenderly to her. 4 He said to his father, "Get me this girl as my wife!"

5 When Jacob heard that his daughter Dina had been defiled, his sons were out herding the cattle, so Jacob restrained himself until they came home. 6 Then Hamor, Shechem's father, went to speak with Jacob. 7 Meanwhile, Jacob's sons, having heard the news, came in from the field. They were grieved and outraged. The man had done a disgraceful thing in Israel by forcing Jacob's daughter to sleep with him. Such a thing ought never be done.

8 But Hamor reasoned with them saying, "The soul of my son longs for your daughter. I pray you give her to him as a wife. 9 Intermarry with us. Give us your daughters and take our daughters for yourselves. 10 Dwell among us; the land is open to you. Live in it, trade in it and acquire property in it."

11 Shechem said to Dina's father and brothers, "Open your hearts, whatever you ask of me is yours. 12 Set the dowry as high as you wish and I will give whatever you say, just give me the girl as my wife."

13 Dina's brothers answered Shechem deceitfully, because he had defiled their sister. 14 They said to him, "We cannot do this thing, to give our sister to a man with a foreskin would be a disgrace to us. 15 We can agree only on one condition, that you become like us, by having every male circumcised. 16 Then we will give you our daughters, taking yours for ourselves; and we will stay with you making one nation. 17 But if you do not listen to us and become circumcised, we will take our sister and go." 18 Their proposal seemed good to Hamor and his son Shechem. 19 The young man did not hesitate about doing this, because he was delighted with Dina. He was the most respected in his father's house.

20 So Hamor and Shechem went to the gate of the city and spoke to the men, saying, 21 "These men are friendly. Let them settle in the region and move freely in it. There is plenty of room here for them; we shall marry their daughters and give our daughters to them. 22 But only on this condition will these men agree to settle with us and become a single nation: that all our males be circumcised like them. 23 Will not the livestock they own, their acquired property, all their animals become ours? Let us comply with them, that they may settle among us." 24 All the men agreed and were circumcised.

25 On the third day, when the men were in agony, Leah and Jacob's sons, Simeon and Levi, Dina's brothers, took their swords and entered the city unsuspected and slaughtered all the males. 26 They killed Hamor and Shechem and seized Dina from Shechem's house and went away.

27 The other sons of Jacob came upon the slain and looted the town where their sister had been defiled. 28 They seized their flocks and herds and donkeys, whatever was in the town and in the field. 29 They carried off all their wealth and their little ones and their wives, looting everything in their houses.

30 Jacob said to Simeon and Levi, "You have stirred up trouble for me, making a stench to the Canaanites and Perizzites, the people settled on this land. There are few of us; they'll gather to destroy me, to extinguish my household."

31 But Dina's brothers replied, "Should our sister be treated like a whore?" ◉◉

William A. Bouguereau, *A Classical Beauty by a Well*

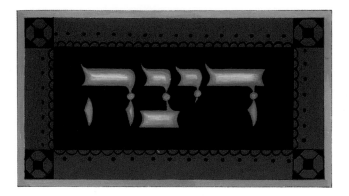

DINA

DINA never spoke in her story, and the voice of the Divine was not heard either. The Twelve Tribes of Israel were named for her brothers, but no tribe was named for Dina. Her story warned that Hebrews were not to trust the peoples among whom they live and that women needed to be restricted in order to be safe. Dina was a tragic heroine.

Dina's violent tale begins just after the family moved back to Canaan. When Dina went out to meet the women in her new town, the prince of the land "seized her and lay with her by force." In an astonishing reversal, her attacker's lust turned to love. Then the pampered prince demanded of his father, "Get me this girl as my wife!" (In the Torah, and even today in many Arab countries, a rapist is vindicated if he marries his victim.)

Many rabbinic midrash use the first verse of Dina's story—"Now Dina, Leah's daughter by Jacob, went out to see the daughters of the land." (Genesis 34:1)—to blame her and to justify keeping women in seclusion. The rabbinic commentators have referred to Dina as "gallivanting" and a "gadabout." Rashi, the revered eleventh-century Talmudic scholar, said that if Dina had stayed at home she would not have been raped, expressing a "she asked for it" mentality that still prevails today.

Women understand that you don't feel at home or truly content in a new place until you've made a woman friend. Dina was the only girl in a large family of boys. She needed the balance and understanding that female friends could offer. It was the pattern of the women in her family to be independent and assertive, not cloistered and passive; women in Haran participated in public life. In the context of Dina's upbringing and family situation, her behavior was perfectly natural—not at all an invitation to rape. Rebecca and Rachel "went out" to the well and found their mates; Dina "went out" to socialize with the Canaanite women and found disaster.

When Jacob learned that his daughter had been raped, he kept silent. He took no action. Dina's father was cold toward her. Where was a father's love for his only daughter? Where was his outrage about her rape? Throughout Dina's tale, Jacob never mentioned her name nor spoke to her. Perhaps she was devalued by her father because she was a girl. Or perhaps he was indifferent to Dina because she was the daughter of Leah, whom Jacob had been tricked into bedding and wedding. And where was Leah? Inexplicably, Leah is absent in the story of her daughter's rape, although she was still alive when her daughter was assaulted. Were Leah's sons Simeon and Levi, Dina's avengers, acting with pent-up rage on behalf of their neglected mother, the unloved wife of Jacob, as well as their sister?

Simeon and Levi took revenge for Dina's rape with vicious brutality. They annihilated an entire community, not just the responsible individual. Their bloody slaughter went far beyond the standard of retribution set later in the Bible as "an eye for an eye and a tooth for a tooth." Dina's is a tale of men vindicating their family honor, a vehicle to show the magnitude of the toughness of the Hebrew tribal brothers. There was no way her brothers would allow the blood of Shechem to mix with theirs. The purity of the Hebrew line was at stake. This time it seems not to be Yah who is in control; it is Simeon and Levi.

Dina's story takes an intriguing twist when we learn that after her brothers killed the prince, "They seized Dina from Shechem's house. . . ." (Genesis 34:26) Why was Dina with Shechem? Could she have forgiven him? Was she in love? Dina and Shechem were, after all, only teenagers at this time. We are left to wonder if she, too, wanted to intermarry—Arab prince and Jewish princess. Was Dina the Jewish Juliet?

Dina's disturbing tale was summed up with her brothers' final comment: "Should our sister be treated like a whore?" (Genesis 34:31) The violent actions of Simeon and Levi marked the first act of war by Hebrews toward the peoples who inhabited Canaan. The storytellers needed a very good reason to justify violence of this intensity.

Dina's story, like the stories of Eve and Rachel, conveys the message that attachment to the feminine will be punished. Eve was banished from Paradise because she listened to the serpent, symbol of Goddess wisdom. Rachel died because she hid the *teraphim,* symbol of the Mother Goddess of fertility. Dina was raped because she went out to connect with the women of the land. But Dina need not be remembered only as a victim. She was a shooting star, a woman who inspired passionate love. We can honor Dina as our sister who exemplified the vital and enduring value of friendship among women. ◉◉

dina

Abel Pann
Genesis 34:26, "Simeon and Levi . . . seized Dina from Shechem's house"

TAMAR
"Date Palm"
Tahmahr

GENESIS : CHAPTER 38

Leah's son, Judah, left his brothers to go south and settle with an Adullamite named Hirah. 2 There a Canaanite named Shua had a daughter and she caught Judah's eye. He asked her to be his wife and came in to her. 3 She became pregnant and gave birth to a son he named Er. 4 Pregnant again, she gave birth to a son she named Onan. 5 And again she conceived and had another son she named Shelah.

6 Judah found a wife for Er, their firstborn; her name was Tamar. 7 But Er was wicked in the eyes of Yah and Yah made him die. 8 Then Judah said to Onan, "Fulfill your obligation to her as a brother-in-law; sleep with her to provide offspring for your brother." 9 But Onan, knowing the child would not count as his, spilt his seed on the ground every time he slept with his brother's wife to keep from producing children for his brother. 10 What he did offended Yah, who caused him to die as well.

11 Then Judah said to his daughter-in-law Tamar, "Go home as a widow to your father, until my son Shelah grows up," for he was thinking, "He too may die like his brothers." So Tamar went to live in her father's house.

12 A long time later, Judah's wife died. Consoled after the period of mourning, Judah went up to Timna to his sheep-shearers, with his friend Hirah the Adullamite. 13 When Tamar was told, "Your father-in-law is on his way to Timna for the sheep-shearing," 14 she took off her widow's garb, covered herself with a veil to disguise herself, and sat down at the entrance gate to Enayim, which is on the road to Timna, for she saw that Shelah was grown up but was not offered in marriage to her.

15 When Judah saw her, he thought she was a harlot, for her face was covered. 16 He went up to her by the roadside and said, "Come now, let me come in to you," not realizing she was his daughter-in-law.

"What will you pay me, for sleeping with you?" she asked.

17 "I personally will send you a kid from my flock," he answered.

But she said, "Only if you give me a pledge, until you send it."

18 He said, "What kind of pledge?"

Emile Jean Horace Vernet, *Judah and Tamar* (detail)

Jacopo Bassano, *Tamar Is Led to the Stake*

She answered, "Your seal-and-cord and the staff in your hand."

He gave them to her, and slept with her, and she became pregnant by him.

19 Then she went home, and taking off the veil, resumed wearing her widow's clothing.

20 Judah sent the kid with his friend the Adullamite, to recover the pledge from the woman. But he could not find her. 21 "Where is the sacred prostitute who was by the roadside?" he inquired of the local people.

"There has been no sacred prostitute in this place," they replied. 22 So he returned to Judah and said, "I couldn't find her. The people who live there said there was no prostitute there."

23 Judah said, "Let her keep what she has, lest we become a laughingstock. Even though you didn't find her, I did send her this kid."

24 Now it was after almost three new moons that Judah was told, "Your daughter-in-law Tamar has played the whore, what's more, she's pregnant from her prostitution."

"Bring her out and let her be set on fire," he said.

25 As she was being brought out, she sent a message to her father-in-law. "I am pregnant by the man who owns these," she said. And she added, "See if you recognize whose seal-and-cord and staff these are."

26 Judah recognized them and replied, "She is more in the right than I. After all I wouldn't give her my son Shelah." And he did not sleep with her again.

27 When the time came for her to give birth, there were twins in her womb. 28 As she was giving birth, one of them put out a hand and the midwife grabbed it, wrapped a scarlet thread around his wrist and said, "This one came out first." 29 Yet he drew back his hand and instead, out came his brother and she said, "With what power he crosses boundaries," and Perez (Breach) he was called. 30 Scarlet around his hand, the brother came out after, to be named for the red thread: Zerah (Bright One). Ꮗ

TAMAR disguised herself as a sacred prostitute and slept with Judah, her father-in-law. She is named for the "date palm," which flowers in the desert and bears fruit that is incomparably sweet. And, indeed, the fruit of Tamar's womb was to be sweet. She was a direct ancestor to the greatest kings of ancient Israel, David, and Solomon. The prophets Samuel, Ezekiel, and Jeremiah predicted that the *Meshiach* (the Anointed One) would be born of the line of David. Tamar was a daring and courageous Canaanite woman who risked death by fire to have a child.

Alone — yet considered married — without status, mate, or children, Tamar was twice widowed and destined for obscurity. Emptiness beckoned. Levirate law of the time required a brother to "marry" (that is, sleep with) the wife of his dead brother in hopes that a son would be conceived to carry on the name of the deceased. Judah's eldest son, Er, had first married Tamar, "But Er was wicked in the eyes of Yah and Yah made him die." (Genesis 38:7) Then Judah's second son, Onan, slept with Tamar, but Onan "spilt his seed on the ground every time he slept with his brother's wife . . . What he did offended Yah, who caused him to die as well." (Genesis 38:9,10) Judah promised his third son, Shelah, to Tamar, but he had no intention of keeping his promise and Tamar knew it. She understood that to Judah she was a reminder of, and perhaps the reason for, the loss of his sons. Did she, too, wonder if she was a curse? Perhaps she did, but she was not willing to passively accept a childless future.

Norma Rosen notes in her book *Biblical Women Unbound:* "Childless women of the Bible generally count on God as a womb-opener. Sarah. Rebekah. Rachel. Hannah. But Tamar does not pray for a child as Hannah does. Or weep or rail and despair as Rachel does. Or resign herself as Sarah

tamar

does. Tamar imagines and invents. She studies the characters of those around her, assumes a character for herself, chooses a setting, devises a plot, and brings it to its completion in dramatic confrontation. In short, she's the performance artist and dramatist of a novel she has written."[7]

Tamar's story recalls a time when the sacred prostitute was part of village life and sexual intercourse was an act of worship of the Feminine Divine. Merlin Stone explains: "In the worship of the female deity, sex was Her gift to humanity. She was the Goddess of Sexual Love and Procreation."[8] Priestesses of the Goddess were called *qedesha*—a word that meant "consecrated woman" but is usually translated as "sacred prostitute." Their sexual energy was considered holy. When the priestess made love with a man, the act was a spiritual sacrament. It was common for married as well as single women to live as priestesses within the temple for periods of time and to follow the sexual customs of Goddess worship. This was a venerated practice, not considered immoral in any way. Given Tamar's Canaanite roots, she may actually have been a *qedesha* at one time in her life. The Bible refers to Tamar as both a *qedesha* and as a *zonah* (a common prostitute, also prevalent in those days), so there is some confusion about exactly what role she was playing. One thing we may be certain of, and that is the lusty atmosphere in which our ancestors lived.

Tamar played the harlot, yet the rabbis considered her a paragon of virtue. Despite prostitution, incest, and adultery, the rabbinic commentary has nothing but praise for Tamar. All the other matriarchs are criticized for various character flaws, but not Tamar. The Zohar, the central text of Jewish mysticism, said that her act "was based on a deeper knowledge" and that she was operating with *"Ruach Hakadosh"* (Blessed Spirit). The Talmud said, "Tamar committed adultery and gave birth to kings and prophets . . . A transgression performed with good intention is better than a precept performed with evil [or no] intention." In the face of death by fire, "her heart was like the heart of a lion," according to the Talmud. Her tact in keeping Judah's indiscretion private is considered a model for all humanity. "It is better for a person to cast oneself into a fiery furnace than to put another to shame in public. Whence do we know this? From Tamar."[9] ❧

Jean Leon Gerome, *Veiled Circassian Lady* (detail)

MIRIAM
"Bitter Sea"
Meeryahm

EXODUS : CHAPTER 1

A new king arose over Egypt who did not know Joseph. 9 He said to his people, "The Israelites are now more numerous than we are. 10 We must deal shrewdly with them, before their numbers increase even further, because if war breaks out, they may join our enemies, fight against us and escape from our land."

11 So they set taskmasters over them to oppress them with forced labor. And they built for Pharaoh treasure cities, Pithom and Raamses. 12 But the more they afflicted them, the more the Israelites multiplied and grew. So that the Egyptians came to dread the Israelites 13 and worked them ruthlessly. 14 They made their lives bitter with hard labor: making bricks, digging mortar, working in the fields—labor was imposed on them without mercy.

15 The king of Egypt said to the Hebrew midwives, one was called Shifrah and the other Puah, 16 "When you deliver the Hebrew women and observe them on the birthing stool, if it is a boy, kill him; but if it is a girl, let her live." 17 The midwives, fearing Elohim, did not obey the king of Egypt; they let the boys live. 18 So the king summoned the midwives and asked them, "Why have you done this? Why have you let the boys live?"

19 The midwives answered Pharaoh, "Because the Hebrew women are not like the Egyptian women; they are like animals. Before the midwife can come to them, they have given birth." 20 And Elohim dealt well with the midwives, and the people increased and became even more numerous. 21 For this Elohim was good to the midwives and gave them households of their own.

22 Pharaoh then gave to all his people this command: "Every boy born of Israel must be thrown into the Nile, but let all the girls live."

EXODUS : CHAPTER 2

There was a Levite woman who was married to a Levite man. 2 She conceived and gave birth to a son. Seeing what a fine child he was, she kept him hidden for three months. 3 When she could hide him no longer, she got a papyrus basket and covered it with tar and pitch. She put the child inside and laid it among the reeds at the river edge. 4 His sister, Miriam, stood at a distance to see what would happen to him.

Abel Pann
Exodus 1:22, "Every boy born of Israel must be thrown into the Nile"

5 Now Pharaoh's daughter went down to bathe in the Nile, while her maids walked along the riverside. She noticed the basket among the reeds and sent her slave girl to fetch it. 6 She opened it and saw the baby. He was crying. She felt compassion for him and said, "This is one of the Hebrew babies."

7 The child's sister then said to the Pharaoh's daughter, "Shall I go and find you a nurse from among the Hebrew women to nurse the baby for you?"

8 "Yes, go," answered Pharaoh's daughter, and the girl went and called the child's own mother. 9 Pharaoh's daughter said to her, "Take this baby and nurse him for me, and I will pay you." So the woman took the baby and nursed him. 10 When the boy grew older, she brought him to Pharaoh's daughter, and he became her son. Pharaoh's daughter named him Moses (One-Who-Draws-Out) and said, "Because I drew him out of the water."

EXODUS : CHAPTER 15

19 When Pharaoh's horses, chariots and horsemen went into the sea, Yah brought the waters of the sea back over them, but the Israelites walked through the sea on dry ground.

20 Then the prophetess Miriam, sister of Aaron, took up a tambourine, and all the women followed her with tambourines and dancing, 21 while Miriam chanted to them:

"Sing to the Yah,
who has triumphed gloriously . . ."

NUMBERS : CHAPTER 12

Now Miriam and Aaron talked against Moses, because of a Cushite woman whom he had married. 2 "Is it only through Moses that Yah speaks?" they asked. "Hasn't the Infinite One spoken through us, too?"

And Yah heard this.

3 Now Moses was a very humble man, more humble than anyone else on the face of the earth. 4 Suddenly Yah called to Moses, Aaron and Miriam. "Come out, all three of you, to the Tent of Meeting." So the three of them came out.

5 Then Yah descended in a column of cloud and stood at the entrance of the Tent and summoned Aaron and Miriam. When the two of them came forward, 6 the Infinite One said:

"Listen!
When a prophet of Yah is among you,
I reveal my being in visions.
I speak through dreams.
7 Not so with my servant Moses;
he is the most faithful of all my house.
8 With him I speak face to face,
clearly and not in riddles.
And the form of Yah is what he beholds.
Why, then, were you not too awestruck to speak against Moses?"

9 Yah's anger burned against them and the Infinite One left them.

previous pages: William Gale, *The Song of Miriam the Prophetess* (detail)

10 When the cloud lifted from over the Tent, look, Miriam was covered with scales, white as snow. Aaron turned toward her and saw that she had leprosy. 11 He begged Moses, "Please my lord, do not lay guilt on us for the sin we have foolishly committed. 12 Do not let her be like a still-born baby, whose flesh is half-consumed when it comes from its mother's womb."

13 So Moses pleaded with Yah, "Oh Elohim, please heal her."

14 Yah replied to Moses, "If her father spat in her face would she not have had to bear her shame for seven days? Have her shut out of the camp for seven days and after that she may be brought back."

15 So Miriam was shut out of the camp for seven days, and the people did not move on until she was brought back.

NUMBERS : CHAPTER 20

Now they came, the Children of Israel, the whole community, to the wilderness of Zin, in the first new moon of the fortieth year, the final year of wandering. And the people stayed in Kadesh. There Miriam died and was buried. ⍥

Sir Lawrence Alma-Tadema, *The Finding of Moses by Pharaoh's Daughter*

MIRIAM'S

MIRIAM'S was a life of extremes: from enslavement to liberation, from ecstatic leadership to the disgrace of ostracism. Miriam was credited with saving Moses and being a prophet but, ultimately, she was struck with leprosy for questioning her brother and suggesting that she was his equal. What unfolds as a story of redemption ends as a tale of betrayal.

Her name means "bitter sea." The bitterness for which Miriam was named has two roots. It recollects the oppression of the Israelites as slaves in Egypt. It also reminds us of Miriam's bitter struggle against exclusion.

Miriam's story begins in an atmosphere of fiendish cruelty toward the Israelites. Pharaoh had decreed, "If it is a boy, kill him; but if it is a girl, let her live." The rabbinic midrash says that Miriam's father so despaired about this decree that he divorced his wife and declared that he would bring no more babies into the world. Miriam told her father, "You are worse than Pharaoh! The king is trying to kill only the boys, you want to do away with the girls, too!" The truth of his young daughter's words convinced the father to remarry Miriam's mother, and their union gave birth to Moses.[10]

As a young girl, Miriam watched over her brother, the infant Moses, when their mother set him afloat upon the Nile in a papyrus basket. Miriam saw to it, with calm courage and impeccable timing, that the Pharaoh's daughter engaged the services of Moses' mother as wet nurse. Later, we meet Miriam again, now known by the name Miriam the Prophet, by the shores of the Red Sea, which opened, like a woman, to birth the Children of Israel into freedom. Miriam and her brothers were divinely selected by Yah to be the leaders of the Israelites in the journey to freedom: "I brought you up from the land of

Egypt, I redeemed you from the house of bondage, and I sent before you: Moses, Aaron and Miriam." (Micah 6:4) It was Miriam's liberation song and the persuasive percussion of her tambourine that led hundreds of thousands of Israelite women through the Red Sea.

Metaphorically, Miriam fulfilled the promise of her first words in the Bible text, spoken to Pharaoh's daughter, herself a woman so exalted and righteous that midrash names her Bat-Yah (Daughter of Yah). "Shall I go and find you a nurse from among the Hebrew women to nurse the baby for you?" Miriam had said. Miriam was the Hebrew woman who sustained the infant nation. The Bible tells us that Israel received a holy gift during the desert wandering: a miraculous well of water that traveled with the Israelites and kept them alive for forty years in the desert. Legend says that Elohim wrought this miracle to honor the merit of the prophetess Miriam. For this reason, the blessed source of water was called "Miriam's Well."[11] It has been described as a mythic eternal source of healing waters, "a miracle-working spring which appears as a fountain of healing and redemption, then vanishes."[12]

Though a gifted leader, Miriam had to struggle against inequality, and her personal story paralleled the story of her entire gender. When Yah asked Moses to come up Mount Sinai, to meet face-to-face, Aaron was invited to accompany him part of the way. Miriam was left behind. When the first census of Israelites was taken (Numbers 1), only the men were counted. In the period after the Exodus, older matriarchal cultural patterns were left behind as patriarchal structure was consolidated. Miriam and, with her, all Israelite women were betrayed. With the giving of the law to Moses at Sinai, Israelite women were cut off from religious leadership and from the most sacred rituals of the faith.

Judith Plaskow, in her book *Standing Again at Sinai,* writes: "There can be no verse in the Torah more disturbing to the feminist than Moses' warning to his people in Exodus 19:15 (as they are preparing to receive the Holy Law), 'Be ready for the third day; do not go near a woman.' For here, at the very moment that the Jewish people stand at Sinai ready to receive the covenant—not now the covenant with individual patriarchs but with the people as a whole—at the very moment when Israel stands trembling, waiting for God's presence to descend upon the mountain, Moses addresses the community only as men. Moses does not say 'Men and women, do not go near each other.' At the central moment in Jewish history, women are invisible."[13]

Moses, Miriam, and Aaron worked together as a family to lead the Israelites from enslavement to freedom. But the story in Numbers 12 diminished Miriam and Aaron's authority and communicated in no uncertain terms that the chosen one was Moses alone. Miriam and Aaron enraged the Divine One when they spoke against Moses: "Now Miriam and Aaron talked against Moses, because of a Cushite woman whom he had married." (Numbers 12:1) Legend says that Miriam and Aaron rebuked Moses on behalf of his wife Zipporah, who complained that once Moses was chosen to receive Divine revelation he refused marital relations. Miriam and Aaron accused their brother of abstaining from conjugal joy only to show how holy a man he was.

Miriam wanted to be recognized as equal to her brother: "Is it only through Moses that Yah speaks? Hasn't the Infinite One spoken through us, too?" (Numbers 12:2) Her question was answered with leprosy. Why so harsh a punishment? Why wasn't Aaron blamed also? Was Miriam an ego-driven diva? Or was she just a woman who had become too influential? Miriam led the Israelite women. To suppress her leadership was to subdue the community she led. Miriam questioned and searched for truth. We must continue to follow her lead.

After being stricken with leprosy, Miriam was shut out of the camp for seven days. But she was not shut out of the hearts of her people. "The people did not move on until she was brought back." (Numbers 20:15) Miriam had waited by the Nile to watch over her baby brother in his ark of reeds. Now, all of Israel waited for the prophetess, the women's leader, to be healed. After she returned, Miriam's voice was never again heard. Her song was silenced.

Yet Miriam's spiritual influence remains. Unlike the matriarchs we have met thus far, Miriam was not chosen to deliver sons: Her mission was to deliver a nation. Her role was spiritual and patriotic, not biological. Miriam stands alone, stands tall, a single independent woman. Today, a cup dedicated to Miriam the prophetess is included on many seder tables, as a tribute to Miriam and as a symbol honoring the renewal that women have brought to Judaism in the last decades of the twentieth century. Miriam embraced spiritual ecstasy and spoke her truth. She was formidable and charismatic, a prophetess, poetess, dancer, musician, and leader. Despite her dark fate, her potent spirit leads and inspires us still. Miriam personifies women's liberation. Much like the salt in a bitter sea, Miriam's tale both stings and heals. ◉◉

James Tissot, *Miriam Shut Out of the Camp* (detail)

DEBORAH
"Bee" *D'vorah*

JUDGES : CHAPTER 4

The children of Israel again did evil in the sight of Yah. 2 So Yah handed them over to King Jabin of Canaan, whose army commander was Sisera. 3 He had nine hundred iron chariots and had oppressed Israel ruthlessly for twenty years. They cried out to Yah for help.

4 Now Deborah, a prophetess, a woman of flames, judged Israel at that time. 5 She sat under the Palm of Deborah, between Ramah and Bethel, in the hill country of Ephraim; and the children of Israel came to her for judgment.

6 She summoned Barak, the son of Abinoam, from Kadesh-Naphtali, and said to him, "Yah, the Elohim of Israel, has commanded: Go march up Mt. Tabor, and take ten thousand men of Naphtali and Zebulun. 7 I will draw Sisera, the captain of Jabin's army, with his chariots and his troops, to the Kishon River and deliver him into your hands."

8 But Barak said to her, "If you will go with me, then I will go. If you won't go with me, then I will not go."

9 And she said, "I will surely go with you; nevertheless, the journey that you take shall not be for your glory, for Yah will deliver Sisera into the hand of a woman." Deborah rose, and went with Barak to Kadesh. 10 Barak summoned Zebulun and Naphtali together to Kadesh. Ten thousand men marched with him; and Deborah also went up with him.

11 Now Heber the Kenite had severed himself from the other Kenites . . . and had pitched his tent by the great oak in Zahneem near Kadesh.

12 When Sisera was told that Barak had gone up Mt. Tabor, 13 Sisera gathered together all of his chariots, nine hundred chariots of iron, and all of his troops and went from Haroset Ha Goyim to the river Kishon.

14 "Arise!" Deborah said to Barak. "This is the day Yah will deliver Sisera into your hands. Yah is marching before you." So Barak charged down from Mt. Tabor followed by ten thousand men, and 15 Yah threw Sisera and all his chariots and army into a panic before Barak's sword. Sisera leapt from

Francesco Solimena, *Barak and Deborah* (detail)

James Tissot, *Jael Smote Sisera and Slew Him*

his chariot and fled on foot, 16 as Barak pursued the chariots and the soldiers as far as Haroset Ha Goyim. All of Sisera's soldiers fell by the sword. No one was left.

17 Sisera, meanwhile, had fled on foot to the tent of Yael, wife of Heber the Kenite. For there was friendship between King Jabin and the family of Heber the Kenite.

18 Yael came out to greet Sisera and said to him, "Come right in, my lord. Don't be afraid." So he entered her tent, and she covered him with a blanket.

19 "Please let me have a little water to drink, for I am thirsty," he said to her. So she opened a skin of milk and gave him some to drink, and covered him again.

20 He said to her, "Stand in the door of the tent, and if someone comes by and asks you if anyone is there, say 'no.'"

21 Then Yael took the tent peg, and took a hammer in her hand, and went softly unto him, and drove the peg into his temple, and fastened it into the ground, for he was fast asleep from exhaustion. Thus he died.

22 Barak came in pursuit of Sisera. Yael went out to greet him. "Come," she said. "I will show you the man you're looking for." He went in with her, and there lay Sisera with the tent peg through his temple—dead.

23 On that day Elohim subdued Jabin the Canaanite King before the Children of Israel.

24 And the hand of the Israelites grew stronger and stronger against King Jabin of Canaan, until they destroyed him.

JUDGES : CHAPTER 5

The Song of Deborah

On that day, Deborah and Barak sang this song:

3 "Listen, you kings! Give ear, you princes.
From me, from me
comes a song for Yah.
I glorify Yah, Elohim of Israel.

6 In the days of Yael, caravans stopped,
and wayfarers went by roundabout paths.
7 The village life in Israel ceased,
ceased 'til I Deborah, arose.
Arose a mother in Israel.

12 Awake, awake, O Deborah!
Awake, awake, lead the chant.
Arise, O Barak,
Take captive your captors . . .

19 The kings came and they fought,
how they fought, those kings of Canaan,
at Tanach, by Megiddo's waters,
but no booty of silver did they take!

20 The stars fought from their heavenly orbit,
against Sisera.

21 The river Kishon swept them away, that ancient river, the river Kishon.
March on, my soul be strong!

deborah

24 Most blessed of women is Yael,
Of tent-dwelling women she is most blessed.

25 Water he asked for, milk she gave him.
In a lordly bowl she brought him curd.

26 Her left hand reached for the tent peg.
Her right hand for the hammer.
She struck Sisera,
she smashed his head.
Yea, she pierced and shattered his temples.

27 At her feet he crumpled, he fell.
Where he sank, there he lay, destroyed.

28 At the window, she leans and watches,
Sisera's mother cries through the lattice,

'Why is his chariot so long in coming?
Why is the clatter of his chariot delayed?'

29 The wisest of her ladies answers, and she to
herself repeats.
30 'Are they not finding and sharing the spoils:
a girl, two girls for each warrior?
Colorful garments as plunder, embroidered scarves
for me?'

31 So may all your enemies perish, Oh Yah!
Let those who love you be like the sun,
when it emerges in all of its strength!"

And the country had peace for forty years.

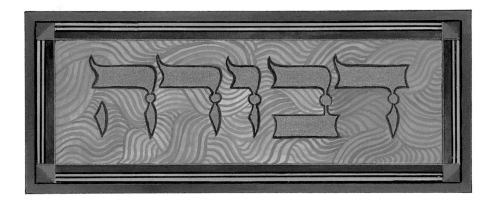

DEBORAH

DEBORAH was a woman of profound influence in ancient Israel. We find her story in the Book of Judges, which chronicles a chaotic and corrupt era, after the Exodus and before the dawn of the Kingdom of Israel. The Israelites proved unable to govern themselves according to the Law of Moses. An angry Yah repeatedly allowed the nation to fall under the control of invaders and adversaries. When the Israelites cried out to Yah for help, the Holy One graciously sent "judges" to deliver Israel from oppression. Deborah was a divine deliverer sent by Yah. She led with courage, strength, and faith.

As her story opens (in English Bible translations), Deborah is introduced as prophetess, judge, and "Lapidote's wife." In Hebrew, another way to translate the words *eshet lapidote* is "woman of flames." One could not create a more apt description of Deborah. As Miriam's element was water, Deborah's was fire: She was the fiery consort of Yah.

Her story draws potency from two sources: the feminine and the Divine. A tremendous storm rendered the Canaanites' iron chariots useless on sodden ground. The foes of the Hebrews were swept away by a swollen river. Two warrior women, manifesting the Goddess traits of motherliness and bloodthirstiness, won the battle. Masculine power is absent in this tale, which was probably written by a woman. The men in this story are weak compared to the women. Barak, a general whose name means "lightning," sounded like a child talking to his all-powerful mommy when he said to Deborah, "If you go with me, then I will go," before he went off to battle. Deborah's answer was, "The journey that you take shall not be for your glory, for Yah will deliver Sisera into the hand of a woman." (Judges 4:8,9) It was Yael who dealt that fatal blow to Sisera. Yael was a black widow spider to Deborah's queen bee.

deborah

Yael's action was set in her tent, which is associated with the womb. Yael nurtured Sisera with milk from a skin. She swaddled him in blankets and synthetic security. Then she struck with lethal power. Her weapons were iconic male symbols: a tent peg and a workman's hammer. It was a gender role-reversal. Yael was the avenger of women raped, enslaved, tortured, and used as spoils of war. This story is not pacifist. It supports the view that sometimes it takes war to make peace. Because Deborah and Yael were warriors, this turbulent tale had a happy ending: "And the country had peace for forty years." (Judges 5:31)

Throughout this story, Deborah was all-knowing and utterly confident. Every biblical woman we've encountered so far was "put in her place" at some point in her story. Not Deborah. From first word to last, Deborah reigns.

The rabbinic interpreters of Torah could not handle the magnitude of Deborah's power. The Talmudic sages labeled Deborah arrogant, haughty, and boastful. Rabbi Hillel said she was punished and the Holy Spirit was taken from her because she boasted that: "I, Deborah, arose a mother in Israel." (Judges 5:7) Rav Nachman said her name was hateful because she was arrogant. Feminist Talmudic scholar Leila Leah Bronner writes: "By analyzing this great biblical figure in terms of the 'unwomanly' trait of arrogance, the rabbis diminish her towering image as a leader. Surprisingly, not one sage came to her defense or suggests a different interpretation. This is not in keeping with Talmudic discussion, in which both pro and con arguments are given."[14]

In modern times, Deborah would be called controlling, a know-it-all. And indeed, she was. A general's job is to be controlling. A prophetess is a know-it-all. Deborah was like "the sun when it emerges in all of its strength." (Judges 5:31) Her mighty spirit invites the warrior woman within us to show herself. Deborah was more than mortal, she was mythic.

Gustave Paul Dore, *Deborah's Song*

DELILAH
"Delicate One"
D' leelah

4 Samson fell in love with a Philistine woman in the Vale of Sorek. Her name was Delilah. 5 And the Philistine rulers came to her and said, "Entice him and find out where his great strength comes from, and how we can overpower him, so we may tie him up and make him helpless. Each of us will give you eleven hundred silver shekels."

6 Delilah said to Samson, "Please tell me what makes you so strong and what it would take to bind and subdue you." 7 Samson answered, "If I were bound with seven fresh bowstrings, which had not been dried, I would become as weak as an ordinary man."

8 So the Philistine chiefs brought her seven fresh, strong tendons, still moist. She bound him with them. 9 Now she had men concealed in her room, and she called out, "Samson, the Philistines are upon you!" He broke the tendons as easily as a string snaps at the touch of a flame. The secret of his strength remained unknown.

10 Then Delilah said to Samson, "You deceived me. And lied to me! Now tell me how you can be tied up." 11 He replied, "If I were bound with new ropes that had never been used, I would become as weak as an ordinary man." 12 So Delilah took new ropes and bound him with them, while the men were concealed in her room. She cried, "Samson, the Philistines are upon you!" But he tore the ropes from his arms as if they were threads.

13 Delilah said, "You've been deceiving me. You've been lying to me. Now tell me what would be needed to bind you." He said, "If you weave seven locks of my hair into the fabric on your loom and tighten it with a peg, I'll become as weak as an ordinary man."

14 She lulled him to sleep, then wove the seven locks of his hair into the warp and tightened them with a peg and shouted, "Samson, the Philistines are upon you!" He awoke from his sleep and pulled out the peg and the loom.

15 Then Delilah said to him, "How can you say you love me when you don't confide in me? This makes three times that you've deceived me and not told me the secret of your great strength." 16 Day after day she nagged him until he was annoyed to death.

Peter Paul Rubens, *Samson and Delilah*

17 At last he confided everything to her. "No razor has ever touched my head," he said. "I have been a Nazarite, dedicated to Elohim, since my birth. If my hair were cut, my strength would leave me and I would become as weak as an ordinary man."

18 When Delilah realized that he had told her the truth, she sent for the Philistine rulers with this message, "Come back once more, for he has confided everything to me." The rulers of the Philistines returned with the money in their hands. 19 Having lulled him to sleep, on her lap, she summoned a man to cut off his seven locks. Thus she weakened him and made him helpless. His strength slipped away. 20 She cried, "Samson, the Philistines are upon you!" He awoke from sleep, thinking, "I shall break free." But he did not know that Yah had left him.

21 The Philistines seized him, gouged out his eyes and brought him down to Gaza in bronze shackles. He became a slave in the prison, grinding grain. 22 But his hair began to grow again.

25 When the Philistines were in high spirits, they shouted, "Bring out Samson to amuse us." Samson was summoned from the prison and he danced for them. Then they made him stand between the pillars. 26 Samson told the boy who was leading him by the hand, "Lead me to where I can feel the pillars that support the temple, so that I may lean against them."

27 Now the temple was crowded with men and women. All the Philistine chiefs were there. On the roof, watching Samson perform, were about three thousand women and men.

28 Samson called to Yah, "Adonai Yah, please remember me and give me strength again, this one time, Oh Elohim, to take revenge on the Philistines with one blow for my two eyes." 29 He embraced the two central pillars on which the temple rested, leaning against them, his right arm around the one and his left around the other.

30 "Let me die with the Philistines," Samson cried. Then he pulled with all his might. The temple came crashing down on the chiefs and all the people in it. Those who were slain by Samson when he died outnumbered those who had been slain by him when he lived. ☙

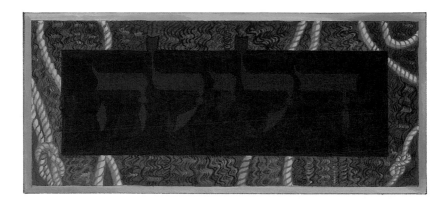

DELILAH

DELILAH, the Scripture's most famous female betrayer, could also be called the dominatrix of the Bible. What else can explain Samson's willingness to submit four times to being tied up by her? Samson was a slave to his uncontrollable passion for her. He was blinded by it, in every sense of the word.

Samson was the Jewish Hercules, a strongman who became a national leader. An angel of Yah had come to Samson's mother—another of the Scripture's barren women—and told her: "You are going to conceive and bear a son. Let no razor touch his head, for the boy is to be a Nazarite of Elohim from the womb on. He shall be the first to deliver Israel from the Philistines." (Judges 13:5)

Samson was extraordinary. As a young man, he killed a fully grown lion with his bare hands. Divine power found expression through Samson's superhuman physical strength. Samson, the prophet, was the penultimate of the judges. During a period when the Philistines dominated the Israelites, Samson led his people for twenty years. He was a trickster who loved to incite the Philistines, a warrior who singlehandedly slew thousands of their men. His weakness was a lust for Philistine women. Delilah was a knock-out. And Samson fell for her.

Delilah was a temptress, but she was not a deceiver. She asked Samson directly what the secret of his strength was. Four times he told her to tie him up in different ways. It's as if he were a willing participant in a bondage game. The game turned deadly when he finally told her the truth. Delilah extracted his secret through nagging: "'How can you say you love me if you don't confide in me?' . . . Day after day she nagged him until he was annoyed to death." (Judges 16:15,16). The message is that loving a woman, especially a non-Jewish one, can be a deadly trap. She will seduce a man, tie him down, then nag him to death.

delilah

The story of Delilah's disastrous seduction of Samson is one of the best-known stories in Western civilization. Like Eve, Delilah is a woman whose story is recognized outside Sunday school. Both stories are used as proof of the untrustworthiness of women. Delilah captivated Samson with her femininity; she was the ultimate femme fatale.

Delilah sold the secret of Samson's awesome strength for a huge sum. It was dangerous work, but she made a fortune. Each of the Philistine lords gave Delilah eleven hundred pieces of silver. Judas betrayed Jesus for only thirty. Delilah worked for the Philistine lords, yet in the end she furthered the cause of Israel's freedom from their rule. "Those who were slain by Samson when he died outnumbered those who had been slain by him when he lived." (Judges 16:30) About three thousand Philistines perished in Samson's suicide mission. We're never told if Delilah died when Samson pulled down the pillars of the temple, crushing all within. Perhaps Delilah escaped that fate because she was working for both sides. Like a skillful double agent, she mysteriously disappeared at the denouement. ⌘

delilah

Paul-Albert Rouffio, *Samson and Delilah*

HANNAH
"Grace"
Chanah

1 SAMUEL : CHAPTER 1

There was a certain man who was from the hill country of Ephraim whose name was Elkanah. 2 He had two wives. One was named Hannah, and the other Peninah. Peninah had children, but Hannah had none.

3 Every year this man would go to Shiloh to sacrifice to Yah.... 4 When sacrifice day came, he would give portions to Peninah and all her sons and daughters. 5 But to Hannah, he would give only one portion. For he loved Hannah, but Yah had closed her womb. 6 To make her miserable, her rival would taunt her because she was barren. 7 This would happen year after year. Whenever she went to the temple of Yah, her rival would provoke her till she wept and could not eat. 8 Elkanah, her husband, said to her, "Hannah, why are you crying? And why aren't you eating? Why are you so downcast? Am I not more to you than ten sons?"

9 Hannah rose after they ate and drank. Now Eli, the priest, was sitting by the doorpost of the temple of Yah. 10 Hannah's soul was deeply pained and she prayed to Yah, weeping bitterly. 11 She made this vow, "Oh, Yah of Hosts, if you would only notice the misery of your servant and remember me. If you will not forget your servant, and give your servant a son, then I will dedicate him to Yah, for all the days of his life, and no razor shall ever touch his head."

12 As she continued praying to Yah, Eli watched her mouth. 13 Hannah was praying in her heart. Her lips moved but her voice could not be heard. Eli thought she was intoxicated. 14 So Eli said to her, "How long will you stay drunk? Sober up!"

15 Hannah answered, "My lord, I am a woman in anguish. I have not had wine nor strong drink; I am pouring out my soul to Yah. 16 Do not regard me as a wicked woman. I have been praying here from the depth of my bitter provocation and my grief."

17 "Go in peace," Eli told her. "And may Elohim of Israel answer your prayer." 18 She replied, "May your servant find favor in your sight." So the woman went on her way. She ate, and her face was no longer sad.

James Tissot, *High Priest and Hannah*

19 Early the next morning, they arose and bowed low before Yah. Then they returned home to Ramah. Hannah lay with Elkanah, and Yah remembered her. 20 It came to pass that Hannah conceived and bore a son. She named him Samuel. "Because I asked Yah for him," she said.

21 Elkanah went up with the entire family, to offer the annual sacrifice to Yah to fulfill his vow. 22 Hannah did not go. "I will not go until after the boy is weaned," she said to her husband. "Then I will take him before Yah, to stay there always."

23 "Do what seems best to you," her husband told her. "Stay here until you've weaned him. May the word of Yah be fulfilled." So the woman stayed home, and nursed her son, until she weaned him.

24 After he was weaned, she took him with her, along with three bulls, an ephah of flour and a skin of wine. And though the boy was still very young, she brought him to the House of Yah in Shiloh.

25 They sacrificed the bull and brought the boy to Eli. 26 She said to him, "Oh, my lord. As you live, my lord. I am the woman who stood beside you here, praying to Yah. 27 I prayed for this child. And Yah gave me what I asked for. I, in turn, lend him to Yah. For as long as he lives, he is lent to Yah." They bowed low before Yah.

And Hannah prayed and said:

"My heart rejoices in Yah.
My horn exalts Yah.
My mouth speaks boldly against my enemies,
For I delight in your deliverance.

2 None is like Yah.
There is none beside you,
No rock like our Elohim.

3 Talk no more with boastful pride.
Don't let your lips speak arrogance!
For Yah is the all-knowing Elohim,
By the Infinite One are actions measured.

4 The bows of the mighty are broken.
The faltering are armed with strength.
5 Those who were full hire themselves out for food,
But those who were hungry hunger no more.
While she who was barren gives birth to seven,
the mother of many is forlorn.

6 Yah slays and makes alive.
Brings down to the grave and raises up.
7 Yah makes poor and makes rich.
Yah humbles. Yah lifts high.

8 Raises the poor from the dust,
Lifts the needy from the dunghill,
seating them with nobility,
in a throne of honor.
For the pillars of the earth are Yah's.
The world is set upon them.

9 The Infinite One will guard the steps of
the faithful,
But the wicked ones will be silenced in darkness.
It is not by strength that one prevails.

10 Those who oppose Yah will be shattered.
The Infinite One will thunder against them
from heaven.
Yah judges the ends of the earth.
The Infinite One endows power to the King,
and exultation to the anointed."

11 Hannah and Elkanah went home to Ramah. The
boy entered the service of Yah under Eli the priest.

18 Samuel, a child wearing a linen loincloth, served
Yah. 19 Each year his mother would make him a
little robe and bring it to him when she made the
pilgrimage with her husband to the annual sacrifice.
20 Eli would bless Elkanah and Hannah and say,
"May Yah grant you an heir in exchange for the one
you have dedicated to Yah." Then they returned
home. 21 Yah was gracious to Hannah. She conceived
and bore three sons and two daughters. Meanwhile,
her son Samuel grew up serving Yah. ◎◎

108

Franck W. W. Topham, *Hannah brings her little son Samuel to Eli the priest* (detail)

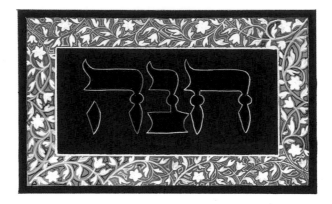

In **HANNAH**, we meet the mother of Jewish spirituality, the woman who teaches us to be fully present, to pray from the heart, and to act with honor. Yearning for a child, suffering from infertility, and tormented by her rival, Hannah entered the sanctuary and pleaded for compassion from the Source of All. "Hannah was praying in her heart." (1 Samuel 1:13) And her heart's cry was heard.

Hannah's name means "grace," which is divine love. Divine love is woven into the fabric of this story, like the robe Hannah made each year and brought to her son Samuel, who lived in the temple with the priest Eli. The Divine One answered the prayer in Hannah's heart. She dedicated her son Samuel to the Divine One as promised. Faith illuminates this tale.

Hannah's prayer was one of the few women's prayers recorded in the Hebrew Bible. It marked a profound shift in Hebrew prayer and in ritual. In Hannah's days, the sanctuary was primarily used for blood sacrifice. Hannah offered her rage as her burnt offering, her tears as her sacrificial lamb, her bitterness as her guilt offering. Hannah's prayer marked the first time that heartfelt spontaneous prayer — "the prayer of the heart" — replaced animal sacrifice as the central act of Jewish worship. Hannah understood that ceremony and slaughter were not substitutes for one's presence in spirit.

Intuitively, Hannah knew how to pray. She worshipped silently, her lips forming words that expressed her truth and her need. Her prayer gave shape to her longings. She allowed her emotions to pour out, and that emotional release opened the gates for holiness to come through.

Three characteristics of heartfelt worthy prayer are gleaned from Hannah: Pray in your heart, allow your lips to form your truth; and concentrate. The heart is honesty with self, the lips are acknowledgment to self and request to the Divine, concentration is focus and willingness to hear. Being fully present both physically and spiritually opens us to connection, understanding, and action.

With focused intention, Hannah pleaded with the Divine. As she connected with Yah, without boundaries of liturgy or convention, she entered an altered state, merging with the Infinite One. Hannah went through a transformation during her prayer. And so did the Hebrew religion. In her humble and courageous way, Hannah challenged the system. With Hannah's prayer, the very heart of Judaism was transformed. ☺☺

hannah

"Cause of Joy"

Avigayil

I SAMUEL : CHAPTER 25

2 A very rich man was in Maon. His possessions and business were in Carmel. He owned three thousand sheep and a thousand goats, which he was shearing in Carmel. 3 The man's name was Nabal, his wife was Abigail. She was a woman of intelligence and beauty, but he was a harsh man, mean and surly.

4 While David was in the wilderness, he heard that Nabal was shearing his sheep. 5 David dispatched ten young men and instructed them, "Go up to Carmel, visit Nabal and greet him in my name. 6 Tell him, 'Long life to you. Peace to your family, peace to all that is yours. 7 I heard that you are shearing. Now when your shepherds were with us, we did not harm them, all the time they were at Carmel nothing of theirs was stolen. 8 Ask your own young men and they will tell you. Now please, receive my men graciously, for we have come on a festive occasion. Please give your servants and your son David whatever you can.'"

9 David's young men delivered his message to Nabal and waited. 10 Nabal retorted, "Who is this David, who is the son of Jesse? 11 Nowadays there are many servants who run away from their masters. Shall I take my bread, my water, and the meat I have slaughtered for my shearers, and give it to men coming from who knows where?"

12 David's men turned around and went back and told him exactly what had been said. 13 David ordered, "Every man, buckle on your sword." They put on their swords and David buckled on his, too. About four hundred men followed David while two hundred men remained with the baggage.

14 One of Nabal's young men told Abigail, "David sent messengers from the desert to greet our master, but he railed at them. 15 Yet David's men were very good to us, they did not harm us, and the whole time we were out in the fields near them nothing was lost. 16 Night and day, all the time we were minding the sheep, they were like a rampart to us. 17 So consider carefully what you should do, disaster is hanging over our whole household. He is such a brute that no one can say a word to him."

Nicolas Vleughels, *Meeting of David and Abigail* (detail)

18 Abigail made haste. She took two hundred loaves of bread, two skins of wine, five already prepared sheep, five measures of roasted grain, a hundred clusters of raisins, two hundred cakes of pressed figs and she loaded them on donkeys. 19 She told her servants, "Go on ahead. I'll follow you." But she did not tell her husband Nabal. 20 She was riding her donkey into a mountain ravine. Behold, David and his men were coming toward her. She met them.

21 Now David had just been saying, "I wasted my time protecting that man's property in the desert, so that he lost nothing at all. He has repaid my goodness with evil. 22 May Elohim deal with David even more harshly if by morning any one of his, who pees against a wall, is still alive."

23 When Abigail saw David, she quickly dismounted from her donkey and threw herself face down before him. 24 Kneeling at his feet she pleaded, "Let me take the blame, my lord. Hear your servant's plea. 25 Don't, please, pay attention to that brute Nabal, for his nature is like his name, 'fool' is his name and a brutal fool he is. As for me, your servant, I did not see the man you sent. 26 My lord, as Yah lives and as your soul lives, by Yah who has kept you from taking revenge with your own hand, may all your enemies and all those who intend to harm you become like Nabal. 27 Let my gift be given to the men in your service. 28 Please pardon your maid's boldness, for Yah will assure you of a lasting dynasty, because you fight Yah's battles and no evil is to be found in you.

29 Should anyone set out to pursue you and seek your life, Yah will keep you safe in the bundle of life, but the lives of your enemies will be flung away, as from a sling. 30 When Yah has fulfilled all the good things promised for you and has made you ruler over Israel, 31 you must have no anxiety, my lord, no remorse over having wantonly shed blood, over having taken revenge. When Yah has brought you success, remember me."

32 David said to Abigail, "Blessed be Yah, Elohim of Israel, who sent you to meet me today. 33 Blessed be your wisdom and bless you for restraining me from bloodshed and revenge. 34 But as sure as Yah Elohim of Israel lives—who has kept me from hurting you—had you not come quickly to meet me, not a single man of Nabal's would be alive in the morning."

35 Then David accepted from her hand what she had brought him. "Go home in peace," he said. "I have listened to you and respect your wish."

36 When Abigail came home to Nabal, he was having a feast in his house, a feast fit for a king. Nabal was in high spirits and very drunk, so she did not tell him anything until morning light. 37 In the morning, when Nabal sobered up and his wife told him all that had happened, his heart died within him and he became like a stone. 38 About ten days later, Yah struck Nabal and he died.

Peter Paul Rubens, *The Meeting of David and Abigail* (detail)

39 When David heard that Nabal was dead, he said, "Blessed be Yah, who championed my cause against the insults of Nabal and held back his servant from wrongdoing. Yah has made Nabal's wickedness rebound on his own head."

40 Then David sent a proposal to Abigail, asking her to be his wife. When David's messengers came to Abigail at Carmel, they said, "David has sent us to bring you to become his wife." 41 She stood up, then prostrated herself on the ground. "Consider me a slave," she said, "to wash the feet of my lord's servants." 42 Abigail rose quickly and rode on a donkey, followed by five maids in attendance. She left with David's messengers and became his wife. ❧

ABIGAIL'S is the Cinderella story of the Scripture. Trapped in an abusive marriage, she bravely snuck out to save her household and won David's heart with her beauty, modesty, and wise actions.

Abigail mastered the blind anger of both her husband, Nabal, a brutish lout, and the poet-warrior King David; in either case, a direct challenge would have produced disaster. Abigail's capability for deflecting anger was outstanding. "Let me take the blame, my lord." (1 Samuel 25:24) These disarming words introduced her plea for peace. Prostrating herself at David's feet, she said, "Please pardon your maid's boldness." (1 Samuel 25:28) Later, her comment in response to his marriage proposal was, "Consider me a slave, to wash the feet of my lord's servants." (1 Samuel 25:41) Why does she sound so excessively submissive? What did the storyteller want her tale to teach us? The lesson is this: In the external world, operate very softly from your core of inner strength. Protect yourself in this way.

The problem of abusive domestic behavior appears eternal. The dynamics of Nabal and Abigail—he grouchy and competitive, she conciliatory and peace loving—are archetypal. Abigail learned diplomacy the hard way. She learned to cultivate patience. She knew that standing up to her abusive husband would provoke him. Her husband's display of bad temper had created a horrendous situation, but she could not confront him. The relief of emotional expression was a luxury that would have destroyed her. Instead, she quietly took positive action to rescue her household. She did not allow her husband to dominate her, but she also knew that she had to act humbly. This was about survival. How she appeared didn't matter. It was what she did that counted.

If Abigail had not taken responsibility for interceding with David, her entire household would have been massacred. She courageously rode alone to meet him. Here was a woman capable of orchestrating a feast for six hundred men — quickly. Abigail knew that fighting occurs when people are hungry or tired. David was a fugitive at this time, living in the hills with his loyal army of six hundred hungry followers. Nabal's nasty dismissal of David's gentle request for food were fighting words, particularly after the many kind acts David's followers had performed toward Nabal's herdsmen. Abigail knew that a satisfying meal could help the process of mediation. Hospitality flowed from Abigail, as it had from Sarah.

She disarmed David with her openness and her willingness to take blame, begging him not to pay attention to her brutal fool of a husband. She also took responsibility for righting the wrong and gave him food, lots of good food. She honored David. She flattered him. And gave him sustenance. Abigail reminded David of the anxiety and remorse he would feel if there were bloodshed, and voiced her concern over the guilt he'd experience if he took revenge. Abigail softened him up. She attracted his eye, fed his body, built up his ego, and she brought him back to his own heart and soul. This humble woman was ultimately more powerful than any man in this story.

Abigail's name means "cause of joy." It felt good to be in her company. Abigail had a tranquil disposition and a wonderful mind. The very first word used to describe Abigail by the Bible text concerned her intellect: "She was a woman of intelligence and beauty." (1 Samuel 2 5 : 3) Abigail came between two men who wanted to fight and she brought peace. Her gentle wisdom prevailed. After she defended her household with hospitality and insight, Yah rewarded her goodness with a fairytale ending to her story. She married the handsome man who would be king. ❧

BATHSHEBA
"Daughter of the Oath"
Batsheva

2 SAMUEL : CHAPTER 11

2 One evening David got up from resting and was strolling on the roof of the royal palace. From the roof he saw a woman bathing. She was very beautiful. 3 David sent someone to learn more about her and was told, "That is Bathsheba, the wife of Uriah the Hittite." 4 David sent messengers to fetch her. She came to him and he lay with her. She had just purified herself after her period. She then returned home. 5 Bathsheba conceived and sent word to David, "I am pregnant."

6 David sent this message to Joab: "Send me Uriah the Hittite." So Joab sent him to David. 7 When Uriah came to him, David asked how Joab was, how the soldiers were faring and how the war was going. 8 Then David said to Uriah, "Go down to your house and bathe your feet." After Uriah left the palace the king sent a present to him.

9 Uriah, however, slept at the palace gate with all of the other officers, and did not go down to his house. 10 When it was reported to David that Uriah had not gone home, he asked, "You just returned from a journey, why didn't you go to your house?"

11 Uriah answered David, "The ark and Israel and Judah are staying in tents, my master Joab and my lord's guards are camped in an open field. How can I go home and eat and sleep with my wife? By your life and the life of your soul, I will not do this."

12 David said to Uriah, "Stay here today and tomorrow I will send you off." So Uriah remained in Jerusalem. 13 The following day, David invited him for food and drink. And David got him drunk. In the evening, Uriah went out to sleep on his mat among his master's soldiers. He did not go home.

14 In the morning, David wrote a letter to Joab which he sent with Uriah. 15 In it he wrote, "Put Uriah in the front line where the fighting is fiercest, and then fall back, so he may be killed."

16 While Joab had the city under siege, he stationed Uriah where he knew there would be the toughest warriors. 17 When the men of the city came out and attacked Joab, there were casualties among David's guards and Uriah the Hittite was killed. . . .

Jan Massys, *David and Bathsheba*

26 Bathsheba heard that Uriah was dead and she mourned for her husband. 27 When the time of mourning was over, David brought her to his house. She became his wife and bore him a son. But what David had done displeased Yah.

2 SAMUEL : CHAPTER 12

Yah sent the prophet Nathan to David. He came to him and said:

"In the same town were two men,
one rich, the other poor.
2 The rich man had flocks and herds,
in abundance.

3 The poor man had nothing, only one little lamb,
only a single little one.
He tended it and it grew up,
together with his children.
It shared his food, drank from his cup,
and slept in his arms.
It was like a daughter to him.

4 When a traveller came to stay,
the rich man would not take anything
from his own flock or herd
to provide for the wayfarer
who had come to him.
So he took the poor man's lamb
and cooked it for his guest."

5 David's anger burned against the rich man and he said to Nathan, "As Yah lives, the man who did this deserves to die! 6 To have done such a thing, to have shown no compassion! He should pay for that lamb four times over!"

7 Then Nathan said to David, "You are that man. . . . 9 You killed the Hittite and took his wife to be your own. 10 For this your household will never be free of the sword, since you showed contempt for me and took the wife of Uriah the Hittite, to make her your wife.

11 "Yah says this: 'I will make calamity rise from within your own household. Before your very own eyes I will take your wives and give them to your neighbor, who will lie with your wives in broad daylight. 12 You acted in secret, but I will do this in the light of the day before all Israel.'"

13 David said to Nathan, "I have sinned against Yah." Nathan replied, "Yah has taken away your sin. You are not going to die. 14 However, since you have outraged Yah by doing this, the child born to you will die." 15 Nathan went home. And Yah struck Bathsheba and David's child, who fell gravely ill.

16 David pleaded with Yah for the child. He kept a strict fast and went home and spent the night lying on the ground. 17 The elders of his household stood around him and tried to get him up, but he refused, nor would he eat. 18 On the seventh day the child died. No one could bear to tell David: "Even when the baby was living, he would not listen to us. How can we tell him the child is dead? He will do something desperate."

bathsheba

Palma Giovane, *The Prophet Nathan Admonishes King David*

19 When David noticed his servants whispering, he perceived that his child was dead. David asked his servants, "Is the child dead?" They replied, "Yes."

20 David got up from the ground, bathed, anointed himself and changed his clothes. Then he went into the sanctuary of Yah and prostrated himself. On returning to his home, he asked for food and ate it.

21 The people of his household said, "Why are you acting like this? When the child was alive, you fasted and wept. Now that the child is dead, you get up and take food."

22 "When the child was alive," he said, "I thought, who knows? Yah may pity me and the child may live. 23 But now that he is dead, why should I fast? Can I bring him back again? I shall go to him but he cannot come back to me." 24 David comforted Bathsheba with lovemaking. She conceived and gave birth to a son, whom she called Solomon.

1 KINGS : CHAPTER 1

1 When King David was old and advanced in years, they put covers on him but could not keep him warm…11Then Nathan said to Bathsheba, the mother of Solomon, "Have you not heard that Adonijah, the son of Haggith, has become king and our lord David does not know it?"…15 Bathsheba went into the aged king's chamber. 16 Bathsheba bowed low and knelt before the king. "What do you wish?" the king asked. 17 She said to him, "My lord, you swore to me by Yah Elohim saying 'Solomon your son shall reign after me and shall sit upon my throne.' 18 But now Adonijah has become king, and you, my lord the king, do not know it…20 Oh king, the eyes of Israel are upon you, to tell them who shall sit on thy throne after you. 21 Otherwise it shall come to pass as soon as the king is laid to rest, I and my son Solomon shall be treated as offenders."

29 And the king gave his oath: "As surely as Elohim, who delivered me from trouble every time, lives. 30 I will surely carry out what I swore to you by Elohim, the ruler of Israel, Solomon your son shall be king after me and he will sit in my throne in my place." ◆

When King David first saw **BATHSHEBA** from the roof of his royal palace, she was bathing in the open, and David was consumed with sexual desire. Although he knew that she was married, he sent for her, and she did not reject him. Bathsheba conceived a baby destined to be their guilt sacrifice—an innocent soul who would live for only seven days. David took the life of Bathsheba's husband and Divine wrath took the life of her first child.

When their adulterous liaison resulted in pregnancy, King David called Bathsheba's husband, Uriah, back to Jerusalem from the front. After engaging Uriah in lengthy conversation about the war, David told him to return home to his wife. But Uriah refused physical contact with Bathsheba; he spent the night in the company of other army officers camped out at the palace gate. When David asked Uriah why he hadn't returned to his house, Uriah answered, "The ark and Israel and Judah are staying in tents. . . . How can I go home and eat and sleep with my wife?" (2 Samuel 11:11) The next day, King David wined and dined Uriah until he was drunk, then again sent him home to his wife. That night, Uriah stayed with his army comrades again. "He did not go home." (2 Samuel 11:13)

Why did Uriah, Bathsheba's husband, a young soldier on sanctioned leave from the battlefront, refuse to return to the arms of his wife? His house was within view. Was Uriah really so loyal to the cause? In truth, it seems that Uriah and Bathsheba's marriage was strained. Perhaps Uriah was angry at her. Perhaps he preferred the company of men. Whatever the true reason for Uriah's lack of passion for Bathsheba, it proved deadly for him. With no way to pretend that Bathsheba was pregnant with Uriah's child, David had her husband eliminated.

bathsheba

Uriah was dispatched to the battlefront, along with this letter to his general: "Place Uriah in the front line where the fighting is fiercest and then fall back, so he may be killed." (2 Samuel 11:15)

Although David was considered the greatest of our kings, a poet and priest and the seminal link to messianic redemption, he was nonetheless human, thus flawed. Motivated by his passion for Bathsheba, he broke three of the Ten Commandments: he coveted his neighbor's wife, he committed adultery; and he committed murder. The prophet Nathan's words to David chill the soul: "For this your household will never be free of the sword, since you showed contempt for me and took the wife of Uriah the Hittite, to make her your wife." (2 Samuel 12:10) David's lust for Bathsheba and his treachery toward Uriah was held against generations to follow. The House of David and the descendants of the Hittites are still not free of the sword.

Bathsheba is barely present in her tale, although she motivates all the action. We learn that she was very beautiful (of course) and that David sent his messengers to fetch her to the royal bedchamber. Feminist Bible scholar Cheryl Exum says: "This is no love story. The scene is the biblical equivalent of 'wham bam, thank you ma'am': he sent, he took, she came, he lay, she returned." [15] Bathsheba is given no voice even as she experienced the deaths of her husband and first baby. When she reappears in her tale, it is once again to make love at David's bidding and to conceive another son. It is as if Bathsheba is only a body, an object of desire, a vessel. She conceives in the first paragraph of her story and conceives again in the last. Bathsheba speaks just three words until the end of her tale, powerful words containing the essence of womanhood: "I am pregnant." (2 Samuel 11:3)

Bathsheba's silence is pregnant also, deep with dark portent and wordless loss. We may speculate on her joys in the arms of a king, but we can also imagine her dark moments of knowing that her adultery caused her husband's murder and her baby's death. Could Bathsheba have refused the king? Did Bathsheba's silence indicate her consent and surrender or the agony of her soul.

When Bathsheba finally spoke up, her intervention determined the future of our people. By insuring that her son Solomon, legendary for wisdom, became king, the influence of a foremother once again decided who would lead the nation. ✍

bathsheba

Marc Chagall, *Bathsheba*

Queen of Sheba
Malkat Sh'va

1 KINGS : CHAPTER 10

The Queen of Sheba heard of Solomon's fame and came to test him with difficult questions. 2 Arriving in Jerusalem with an enormous caravan, camels laden with spices and immense quantities of gold and precious jewels, she came to Solomon and talked with him about all that she had in mind. 3 Solomon had answers for all her questions. There were none too difficult for him to answer.

4 When the Queen of Sheba perceived how very wise he was, and saw the palace he had built, 5 and the food on his table, the accommodations for his officials, the organization of his staff, and the way they were dressed, his wine service, and the burnt offerings which he presented in the Temple of Yah, it left her breathless.

6 "The reports I heard in my own country about you and your wisdom were true, then," she told the king. 7 "Until I came and saw with my own eyes, I did not believe them. But I didn't hear the half of it.

Your wisdom and wealth surpass everything I was told. 8 Your men are happy; those in your presence, hearing your wisdom, are joyful. 9 Praise Yah, your Elohim, who has delighted in you and set you on the throne of Israel! Because of Yah's infinite love for Israel, the Holy One has made you king to maintain justice and righteousness."

10 She presented the king with a hundred and twenty talents of gold and great quantities of spices and precious stones. Never again did such a wealth of spices arrive as that which the Queen of Sheba gave to King Solomon. . . .

13 King Solomon, in turn, gave the Queen of Sheba gifts from his royal bounty, as well as all that she desired and asked for. Then she went home to her own country, she and her entourage. ◉◉

Rudolf Ernst, *The Queen of Sheba*

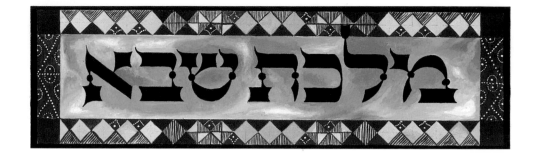

The **QUEEN OF SHEBA** was the epitome of sovereign power. Only thirteen verses form the tale of this wise woman of color, yet her name remains a household word. A courageous seeker, she traveled a great distance to experience the legendary wisdom of Solomon with her own penetrating mind. Fabulously wealthy, she gave Solomon the equivalent of four million dollars (one hundred and twenty talents of gold), rare spices, and precious jewels. Solomon and the Queen met as equals. Theirs was a meeting of minds and more. The queen came to Israel as a worshipper of the sun. She went home knowing the Divine One.

"The Queen of Sheba heard of Solomon's fame and came to test him with difficult questions." (1 Kings 10:1) Her tale stresses the importance of seeking. By following the quest of her heart and by asking forthright and probing questions, the queen gained answers and achieved true satisfaction. She valued wisdom above all. The queen understood that true knowing came only with direct experience: "Until I came and saw with my own eyes, I did not believe them." (1 Kings 10:7)

But her visit was not merely a search for knowledge. The Queen of Sheba had another agenda for establishing an alliance with Solomon. As a head of state, she was leading a crucial trade delegation. Southern Arabia was then, and is now, a major export region for spices. "Never again did such a wealth of spices arrive as that which the Queen of Sheba gave to King Solomon." (1 Kings 10:10) From the time that camels were first tamed and trained—in about 1,000 B.C.E.— caravans carrying precious spices traveled overland from Southern Arabia, on the

Incense Road, which ended in Israel. Whether the caravans would be allowed to continue on their journey through Israel, to Egypt, Phoenicia, and Syria, depended on Solomon. The economic viability of her nation was dependent on the Queen of Sheba's establishing a warm and enduring relationship with King Solomon.

And warm it was. The Queen of Sheba's tale is spare, sculpted, and rich with erotic metaphor. King Solomon adored women. Scripture tells us that King Solomon — a legendary lover — had a harem of seven hundred wives and three hundred concubines. The queen's encounter with Solomon "left her breathless." And Solomon's gifts to her clearly went beyond the material: he gave her "all that she desired and asked for." (1 Kings 10:13)

As for enduring: The meeting of King Solomon and the Queen of Sheba had consequences that have linked Israel and Ethiopia for three thousand years. Ethiopians claim the Queen of Sheba as their own legendary Queen Makeda, and their folklore says the powerful queen left Jerusalem carrying King Solomon's child. On the morn of her departure, according to legend, King Solomon gave the Queen of Sheba a ring with a luminous black stone that had a lion of Judah engraved on it. He told her to give it to their firstborn child. When their child, a boy named Menlik I, put Solomon's ring on his finger, he felt a surge of electric burning energy suddenly coursing through him.[16] Menlik later returned to Jerusalem, stole the ark from the Temple and brought it to the temple at Aksum in Ethiopia, along with an entourage of Hebrew aristocrats who founded the Ethiopian state. The most sacred object of the Hebrew Bible, the stone tablet inscribed with the Ten Commandments and carried down from Mount Sinai by Moses, is believed to be in the temple of Aksum to this day.

Solomon's sacred ring was handed down through countless generations of the Ethiopian ruling family until it was given to the Emperor Haile Selassie — also called Ras Tafari — at his coronation in 1930. Selassie is revered by Rastafarians as the seventy-second and last in a line of human reincarnations of the Divine that included Abraham, Moses, Aaron, David, Solomon, and Jesus of Nazareth. After the death of Selassie, his son gave Bob Marley the ring. "Ya know," Bob told his mother, Cedella, "sometimes dis ring, it burn my finger like fire."[17] The prophet of "One Love," whose music inspires and transcends all boundaries and borders, was buried wearing this mystical ring on his finger.

The Queen of Sheba exemplified the ultimate in diplomacy, power, and autonomy. Yet most people associate the name of the Queen of Sheba with the mocking question: "Who do you think you are, the Queen of Sheba?" This cliché is intended to keep women "in their place." Associated with acting pretentiously, it warns against striving too hard. Yet the Queen of Sheba was not unduly proud; she was complex and effective. The Queen of Sheba was the only

Tintoretto, *The Queen of Sheba before King Solomon* (detail)

one of Solomon's women who was not owned by him, she was his counterpart, his equal. The name of the Queen of Sheba—a woman equal to King Solomon in every way—should be reclaimed with pride, not tarnished by fear of feminine power. ◉◉

JEZEBEL
"Chaste"
Eezehvel

1 KINGS : CHAPTER 16

29 Ahab became king of Israel and reigned for
twenty-two years in Samaria. 30 And Ahab did evil
in the sight of Yah, more than all who preceded
him. 31 It came to pass, as if it were a light thing,
that he followed the sinful example of Jeroboam.
He married Jezebel daughter of Ethbaal, king of
the Phoenicians, and he started to serve Baal and
worship him. 32 Ahab erected an altar to Baal in the
temple of Baal which he built in Samaria. 33 And
Ahab also made a sacred Asherah pole. He did more
to vex Yah, Elohim of Israel, than all the kings of
Israel before him.

1 KINGS : CHAPTER 18

4 When Jezebel was annihilating the prophets of
Yah, Obadiah took a hundred prophets and hid
them, fifty at a time, in a cave, and gave them food
and water. . . .

22 Elijah said to his people, "I am the only prophet
of Yah left, while the prophets of Baal are four
hundred and fifty men.". . .

40 Elijah said, "Seize the prophets of Baal, let not a
single one get away." They seized them: and Elijah

took them down to the Wadi Kishon and
slaughtered them there.

1 KINGS : CHAPTER 21

Naboth of Jezreel had a vineyard close to the palace
of Ahab king of Samaria. 2 Ahab said to Naboth,
"Give me your vineyard so I may have it for a garden
of herbs since it is right next to my palace. I will
give you a better vineyard in exchange, or if you
prefer, I will pay you whatever its value." 3 But
Naboth replied, "Yah forbid that I should give up
to you what I have inherited from my ancestors."

4 Ahab came into his house sullen and resentful
because of Naboth's answer. He lay on his
bed and turned his face away and would not eat.
5 Jezebel came to him. "Why are you so depressed,"
she said, "that you won't eat?" 6 He told her,
"I spoke to Naboth and proposed that he sell me
his vineyard or if he preferred I would give him
another vineyard in exchange. But he answered,
'I will not sell you my vineyard.'" 7 Jezebel said,
"Some king of Israel you are! Brighten up and eat,
I will get the vineyard of Naboth the Jezreelite."

John Byam Liston Shaw, *Jezebel*

jezebel

8 So she wrote letters in Ahab's name and sealed them with his seal, sending them to the elders and nobles of Naboth's town. 9 She wrote in the letters, "Proclaim a fast and seat Naboth in a prominent place among the people. 10 Seat two scoundrels opposite him who will accuse him saying, 'You have cursed Elohim and the king.' Then take him out and stone him to death."

11 The elders and nobles who lived in Naboth's town did as Jezebel directed in the letters she had written and sent to them. 12 They proclaimed a fast and seated Naboth at the front of the assembly. 13 The two scoundrels came and sat opposite him. They confronted him and charged, "Naboth has cursed both Elohim and the king." Then they carried him outside and stoned him to death. 14 Word was sent to Jezebel: "Naboth has been stoned and is dead." 15 As soon as Jezebel heard that Naboth had been stoned to death, she said to Ahab, "Go now and take possession of the vineyard of Naboth the Jezreelite which he refused to sell you, for Naboth is no longer alive, he is dead." 16 When Ahab heard that Naboth was dead, Ahab set out for the vineyard to take possession of it.

17 Then the word of Yah came to Elijah the Tishbite. 18 "Arise, go down to meet Ahab king of Israel who is in Samaria. You shall find him in Naboth's vineyard; he has gone down there to take possession of it. 19 Say to him, 'Thus says Yah: Have you not killed a man and taken his property? Thus says Yah: In the very place where the dogs lapped up Naboth's blood the dogs will lap up your blood too.'"

20 Ahab said to Elijah, "So you have found me, my enemy?"

"Yes, I found you," Elijah replied, "because you have committed yourself to doing what is evil in the sight of Yah. 21 I will bring disaster down upon you. I will sweep away your descendants and wipe out every person who pisses against the wall, slave or freeman. . . .

23 "And Yah has also spoken concerning Jezebel. 'The dogs will devour Jezebel in the field of Jezreel. 24 All of Ahab's line who die in the town shall be devoured by dogs, and all who die in the open country shall be devoured by birds of the sky.'"

25 Indeed there was never anyone like Ahab, who committed himself to do evil in the sight of Yah, urged on by Jezebel.

2 KINGS : CHAPTER 9

30 When Jezebel heard that Jehu had come to Jezreel, she painted her eyes with kohl and adorned her head. She appeared at the window. 31 As Jehu entered the gate, she called out, "Is all well, Zimri, murderer of your master?" 32 He looked up at the window and said, "Who is on my side, who?" Two or three eunuchs looked down at him. 33 "Throw her down," Jehu said. So they threw her down; and her blood splattered on the wall and on the horses as they trampled her.

34 Then he went inside and ate and drank. He said, "Attend to that cursed woman and bury her, for she was a king's daughter." 35 So they went to bury her; but all they found of her were her skull, feet and hands.

Thomas Matthews Rooke, *King Ahab's Coveting: Ahab and Jezebel*

36 They went back and reported to Jehu. And he said, "It is just as Yah spoke through Elijah the Tishbite: The dogs shall devour the flesh of Jezebel in the field of Jezreel. 37 The carcass of Jezebel shall be as dung on the ground in the field of Jezreel, so that not one will be able to say, 'This was Jezebel.'" ❧

JEZEBEL was a defiant queen of Israel. Considered the epitome of an evil woman, she slaughtered many Hebrew prophets and belittled the Divine One as only a local "god of the land." The gruesome murder of Jezebel was intended to not only punish a cruel queen but also to eliminate paganism. Her tale was a warning to all those who revered the Goddess.

Jezebel was a Phoenician princess who came to Israel through an arranged marriage. Her parents were the king and queen of Sidon, as well as high priest and priestess of the religion of the goddess Asherah and of Asherah's consort Baal. Both Jezebel's foreign origins and her faith were strikes against her. Not only did Jezebel embrace paganism, she encouraged her husband, King Ahab, to do the same. Jezebel was a formidable woman, clearly much stronger than her Israelite husband. That was another strike against her.

From the days of Sarah through the time of kings, worship of the Goddess was part of the spiritual life of the Hebrew tribes. Throughout Judges and Kings, the Hebrews are said to be doing what was evil in the sight of Yah. This "evil" was their continued devotion to the worship of Asherah and Baal. The Bible repeatedly refers to sacred poles constructed to honor Asherah, the Great Mother. Most of the Hebrew kings, from Solomon on, intermarried with neighboring royalty and paid homage to the religion of their wives. The Bible says, "Solomon followed Asherah the goddess of the Phoenicians." (1 Kings 11:5) "Ahab also made a sacred Asherah pole. He did more to vex Yah, Elohim of Israel, than all the kings of Israel before him. . . . Indeed there was never anyone like Ahab, who committed himself to do evil in the sight of Yah, urged on by Jezebel." (1 Kings 16:33, 21:25)

Elijah was a zealous prophet intent on uprooting pagan worship and determined to crush Jezebel. In *Biblical Literacy,* Rabbi Joseph Telushkin writes: "It comes as a shock to turn to the biblical texts in which Elijah appears, only to learn that the traditional kindly and lovable prophet bears no relationship to the Elijah of flesh and blood. The most furious and confrontational of the prophets, Elijah may well be the Bible's angriest figure." [18]

Jezebel lived in a time of escalating religious rivalry and war. Incidents of antagonism between Elijah and Jezebel are reported throughout 1 and 2 Kings. Jezebel annihilated prophets of Yah. (1 Kings 18:4) Elijah slaughtered four hundred and fifty prophets of Baal. (1 Kings 18:40) Both Jezebel and Elijah were more than a tad bloodthirsty, but Elijah's name is glorified and hers is reviled. Elijah's victory over Jezebel should be viewed as a triumph for patriarchal religion.

The ancient female religion for which Jezebel stood—with its accompanying autonomy for women—was an offense to the Hebrews. In the Goddess-honoring religion, priestesses were not under the control of men. Kinship was traced matrilineally. The *qedesha* lived in self-supporting temple communities and raised their children together. The proudly sexual priestesses owned property, had legal rights, and were free to relate with many men.

The Israelites introduced a patriarchal system that would closely control women sexually and economically. Each woman belonged to one specific man, first her father and then her husband. From the time of Moses, the marital virginity and sexual fidelity of women was written into law. Sex outside marriage—for women—was punishable by death.

The story of Ahab and Jezebel's expropriation of Naboth's vineyard provides the justification for Jezebel's murder, but this story may have been revised. As author Merlin Stone points out: "Jezebel's supposed crime, that of starting a rumor that resulted in the death of a man, becomes questionable when we realize that it was her husband who actually desired the dead man's property and it was with letters signed and sealed with Ahab's name that she was accused." [19] Israeli Bible scholar Alexander Rofe says that the present account reworks an older story in which Ahab, not Jezebel, was solely responsible for Naboth's death. Rofe believes that four centuries after the story of Jezebel was written, a biblical editor intent on attacking intermarriage shifted the blame to Jezebel to prove the evil of foreign wives. [20]

Jezebel is mistakenly remembered as a harlot because she painted her face before going to her doom. Jezebel's final act was to ring her eyes with kohl and adorn her hair. She prepared to look her best, as any royal person would before an encounter with the public. In addition to being considered a seductress because of her association with the sexual customs of the Goddess religion, Jezebel is thought of as a harlot because, in sixteenth century England, painting the face was evidence that a woman had loose morals.[21] It was during that time that *jezebel* came to mean "a wicked woman."

When Jezebel was thrown to the dogs, a piece of all women's dignity went with her. Her story ends with the words, "The carcass of Jezebel shall be as dung on the ground in the field of Jezreel, so that not one will be able to say, 'This was Jezebel.'" (2 Kings 9:37) Substitute in your mind the words "the Goddess" for "Jezebel" in this last verse of her tale, and you have a description of the intention to wipe out worship of female divinity.

We cannot excuse all that Jezebel was said to have done, but neither should we automatically condemn her. Judgment and condemnation of women comes far too easily. Does she deserve her reputation as a slut? Is it fair that her name be forever associated with the tawdry and the wicked? Certainly she was violent and manipulative. But, her main crime was that she represented worship of the goddess Asherah. In Jezebel, a Phoenician warrior-queen and high priestess, we find strength and faithfulness to the religion of her parents. ◑◡

jezebel

Thomas Matthews Rooke, *King Ahab's Coveting: Ahab and Jezebel,*
Jezebel thrown to her death by two eunuchs, on the order of Jehu

RUTH
"Friend"
Root

NAOMI
"Pleasantness"
Naome

RUTH : CHAPTER 1

Now it came to pass, in the days when judges governed, that there was a famine in the land. So a woman and man of Bethlehem in Judah went to sojourn in the Moab with their two sons. 2 The man was Elimelech and the woman Naomi, their two sons were Mahlon and Chilion. 3 Naomi's husband died, and she was left with her two sons. 4 One married Orpah and the other Ruth, Moabite women, and they lived there for about ten years.

5 Mahlon and Chilion then both died too. Naomi was bereft of her two sons and her husband. 6 She decided to return from Moab with her daughters-in-law, for she heard that Yah had visited her people and given them bread. 7 With her two daughters-in-law, she left the place where she had been living and set out on the road back to Judah.

8 Then Naomi said to her two daughters-in-law, "Turn back, each of you, to her mother's house. 9 May Yah show you faithful love, as you have done with those who died and with me. May Yah grant you happiness in the home of other husbands." She kissed them and they cried 10 and said to her, "We will go back with you to your people."

11 "Go home, my daughters," Naomi replied. "Why come with me? Have I any more sons in my womb to become your husbands? 12 Go back, my daughters, go, for I am too old to marry again. Even if I thought there was still hope for me. If I could take a husband tonight and bear more sons, 13 would you wait for them to grow up? Would you refuse to marry for their sake? Oh no, my daughters, I am bitterly grieved for you that the hand of Yah has struck out against me."

14 They wailed, Orpah kissed her mother-in-law and left. But Ruth clung to her. 15 Naomi said, "See, your sister-in-law has gone back to her people and to her gods. Go follow her."

16 Ruth replied, "Do not urge me to leave you or to turn back from you.
For wither thou goest, I will go;
Wherever you stay, I will stay.
Your people shall be my people,
and your Elohim my Elohim.
17 Where you die, I shall die,
and there I will be buried.
Thus and more may Yah do to me if anything but death parts me from you."

William Blake, *Naomi entreating Ruth and Orpah to return to the Land of Moab* (detail)

18 When Naomi saw how determined Ruth was to go with her, she said no more. 19 The two journeyed until they came to Bethlehem. When they arrived, the whole town buzzed with excitement, and the women said, "Can this be Naomi?"

20 "Do not call me Naomi. Call me Mara because Shaddai has made my life very bitter. 21 I went away full and Yah has brought me home empty. Why then call me Naomi, since Yah is against me and Shaddai has made me wretched?" 22 This was how Naomi came home with her daughter-in-law, Ruth the Moabite. They arrived in Bethlehem at the beginning of the barley harvest.

RUTH : CHAPTER 2

Now Naomi had a kinsman on her husband's side, a mighty man of wealth. His name was Boaz. 2 Ruth the Moabite said to Naomi, "Let me go into the fields and pick up the leftover grain behind someone who will show me kindness."

"Go daughter," Naomi replied.

3 So Ruth went out to glean in the fields behind the reapers. Luck led her to the part of the field belonging to Boaz. 4 Boaz, as it happened, had just come from Bethlehem. "Yah be with you," he said to the reapers. "Yah bless you," they replied. 5 Boaz asked his servant in charge of the reapers, "Who is that young woman?"

6 The servant answered, "The girl is the one who came back from Moab with Naomi. 7 She asked me, 'Pray let me glean, behind the reapers, and pick up what falls from the sheaves.' She's been working from morning till now, with scarcely a rest."

Thomas Matthews Rooke, *The Story of Ruth: Ruth and Boaz*

8 Boaz said to Ruth, "Listen to me, daughter. Don't go to glean in another field. Stay close by my work-women. 9 Keep your eyes on where they're reaping and follow behind them. I have forbidden the men to touch you. When you're thirsty, go to the water jars and drink."

10 Ruth bowed her face to the ground and said, "Why are you so kind to notice me — a foreigner?"

11 Boaz answered, "I heard what you did for your mother-in-law after the death of your husband, how you left your own father and mother, and the land of your birth, and came to a people you had not known before. 12 May Yah, Elohim of Israel under whose wings you have come for refuge, reward you for what you have done."

13 She answered, "May I find favor in your sight. For you have comforted me and spoken kindly, my lord, though I am not one of your work-women."

14 When it was time to eat, Boaz said to her, "Come over here and have some bread. Dip your morsel in the vinegar." So she sat beside the harvesters. He gave her roasted grain and she ate her fill and had some left over.

15 When she got up to work again, Boaz told his workers, "Let her glean among the sheaves themselves. Do not embarrass her. 16 Be sure to pull out some grain from the bundles, and leave them for her to pick up. Don't reproach her."

17 She gathered grain until evening. Then she threshed what she had gleaned. It came to about a bushel of barley. 18 Taking it with her, she returned to town and gave it to her mother-in-law. 19 Her mother-in-law said, "Where did you glean today? Where did you work? Bless the man who noticed you."

"The name of the man with whom I worked," Ruth told her, "is Boaz."

20 "Blessed by Yah is he who does not withhold love from the living or dead," Naomi said to her daughter-in-law. "This man," she added, "is closely related to us. He is a kinsman-redeemer."

21 Ruth the Moabite said, "He told me, 'Stay close to my workers until they are finished harvesting all my grain.'"

22 Naomi told her, "It is best for you, my daughter, to go with his workers, because in some other field you might be molested." 23 So Ruth stayed close to Boaz's work-women and gleaned until the barley and wheat harvests were finished. And she lived with her mother-in-law.

RUTH : CHAPTER 3

One day, Naomi said to Ruth, "My daughter, I seek security for you, so that you will be happy. 2 Is not Boaz, whose women you worked with, our relative? He is winnowing barley tonight at the threshing floor. 3 So bathe, perfume yourself, dress-up and go down to the threshing floor. Don't let him recognize you while he is still eating and drinking. 4 But when he lies down, note the place where he lies. Go over and uncover his feet. And lie down. He will tell you what you shall do."

5 Ruth said, "I will do whatever you tell me."

6 So she went down to the threshing floor and did everything Naomi had instructed her to do. 7 After Boaz had eaten and drunk, his heart was merry. He lay down beside the mound of grain. And she came softly and uncovered his feet and lay down.

8 In the middle of the night, the man startled awake to discover a woman lying at his feet. 9 "Who are you?" he asked. And she replied, "I am Ruth. Spread your wing over your handmaiden, your cloak over your servant, for you are next of kin."

10 "Yah bless you, daughter," he said. "Your latest loving-kindness is greater than the first. For you have not turned to younger men, whether poor or rich. 11 Don't be afraid. I will do for you whatever you ask. All the people in this town know that you are a worthy woman. 12 It's true that I'm your close relative. But there's one closer kin than I. 13 Stay for the night. When morning comes, if he will act as your kinsman, good! Let him redeem you. But if he does not wish to do so, then as Yah lives, I will redeem you. Lie down until morning."

14 So she lay at his feet until dawn, but rose before the hour that one could recognize another. He thought, "It must not be known that this woman came to the threshing-floor." 15 And he said, "Hold out the shawl you're wearing." She held it out, while he poured out six measures of barley. He put it on her back and off she went to town.

16 When Ruth came home, her mother-in-law said, "How did it go, my daughter?" She told her everything Boaz had done for her. 17 "He gave me six measures of barley, saying to me, 'Do not go back to your mother-in-law empty handed.'"

Z. Raban, *Boaz wakes to find Ruth at his feet*

18 Naomi told her, "Do nothing, daughter, until you see how things turn out. Surely he will not rest until he has settled the matter this very day."

RUTH : CHAPTER 4

Meanwhile, Boaz went up to the town gate and sat, and the kinsman he had mentioned came by. Boaz called to him, "Here, my friend, come and sit down." So he came over and sat. 2 Boaz then selected ten of the town's elders and said, "Sit here." And they did so. 3 Then he said to the kinsman, "Naomi, who has returned from Moab, is selling the piece of land that belonged to our kinsman Elimelech. 4 I thought I should disclose this matter to you and say, 'Buy it in the presence of those seated here and in the presence of the elders of my people. If you are willing to redeem it, do so. But if you will not redeem it, then tell me, so that I know. For I am the only one who has the right to redeem besides you, I am next in line.'"

The man said, "I will redeem it."

5 Boaz continued, "On the day you buy the field from Naomi and Ruth, you also acquire Ruth the Moabite, the widow of the deceased, to restore the name of the dead to his estate."

6 At this, the man with the right of redemption replied, "Then I cannot redeem it because I might jeopardize my own inheritance. You redeem it yourself. I cannot do it."

7 Now, in former times, it was the custom in Israel to validate a matter of redemption or inheritance by taking off a sandal and giving it to another. This was the method of legalizing transactions in Israel.

ruth
naomi

8 So when the kinsman said to Boaz, "Buy it for yourself," he pulled off his sandal.

9 Then Boaz declared to the elders and to all of the people there, "You are witnesses today that I am acquiring, from Naomi, all that belonged to Elimelech and his two sons. 10 I am also taking Ruth the Moabite as my wife. . . ."

11 All the people at the gate answered, "We are witnesses." And the elders said, "May Yah make the woman about to enter your family like Rachel and Leah who together built the house of Israel. May you grow mighty in Ephrat, and be famous in Bethlehem. 12 Through the children Yah will give you with this young woman, may your family be like the house of Perez, son of Tamar and Judah."

13 So Ruth and Boaz married. When they came together, Yah made her conceive and she bore a son.

14 And the women said to Naomi, "Bless Yah, who has not left you without a kinsman-redeemer. May his name be praised in Israel. 15 This child will renew your life and nourish you in your old age; for your daughter-in-law who loves you and is better to you than seven sons, has given birth to him." 16 Naomi took the child and held him to her heart. It was she who looked after him. 17 The neighbor-women gave him a name. They said, "A son has been born to Naomi!" And they called him Obed. This was the father of Jesse, the father of David. 🏵.

ויאמר הגאל לבעז קנה־לך וישלף נעלו

Z. Raban, *Boaz pulled off his sandal*

The **BOOK OF RUTH** is an exquisite tale about the bond between women. The narrative is unique in Scripture because it centers around a female family struggling for survival in a man's world. It is a story of women's culture and women's values. It is about absolute commitment, embracing connection, and love as a spiritual path.

Ruth's story is a prism that contains and refracts the tales of many biblical ancestors. Her spiritual journey, like those of Sarah, Abraham, Jacob, and Rebecca, demanded that she leave the security of homeland and kin. At her moment of truth, she repeated Rebecca's exact words, "I will go!" Her destiny with Naomi was as intimately intertwined as Rachel's was with Leah's. She joined Sarah, Rebecca, Rachel, and Hannah in the struggle from infertility to motherhood. Her son, like Rachel's, was born in Bethlehem, a place resonant with sacred birth. Like all the foremothers, Ruth was blessed with daring, resilience, and profound insight.

Naomi is the ancestress who guides us through the terrain of loss. Within the first five lines of her story, she was bereft. Naomi endured the death of the land, her husband, her progeny, her fertility, and her hope. Battered by life, she was on a grueling voyage through a tunnel of pain.

When Naomi returned to Judah, she was greeted by the women of Bethlehem. Naomi cried out to her community of women. She told them that she was once full, but now was empty. Yet her emptiness proved alive with possibility. The Divine blessed her with exactly what she needed to be healed: intimate loving companionship, a caring community of women, and a grandchild. Naomi's pilgrimage took her from bitterness to bliss.

Underlying the plot structure is a sensuous journey, from dry places to moist ones. Wisewoman Naomi counseled Ruth in eroticism. She told Ruth to anoint herself and to lie next to Boaz and uncover his feet. Ruth asked Boaz to spread his cloak over her. Feet are a biblical euphemism for the male sexual organ. "Spreading one's cloak over" are words for sexual intercourse. Sex is a sacred, soulful force in this tale.

Ruth and Naomi were united in loss, yet they were an unlikely pair. Ruth came from a people whom the Israelites despised and considered morally depraved. The Moabites descended from the incestuous liaison of Lot's older daughter with her father, following the destruction of Sodom and Gomorrah. The distrust the Hebrews felt toward the Moabites was intensified when the Moabites refused the Israelites water and bread during the long, thirsty flight from enslavement in Egypt. Adding insult to injury, the Moabites sent a pagan prophet to curse their Israelite cousins. The Torah expressly forbade the Children of Israel to marry Moabites.

But the purity of Ruth's soul outweighed her genealogy. Her book says that love transcends law. It teaches that commitment to a set of ideals is more important than biological descent. It asks us to accept the dedicated convert as kin.

Ruth's book, also called the Book of Lovingkindness, is read year after year on Shavuot, the ancient holiday that celebrates late spring harvest and the giving of Torah. The link between Ruth and the Torah goes to the very heart of Torah. In the immortal words of Rabbi Hillel, "Torah is based on three things: Do justice. Love mercy. Practice lovingkindness."

Ruth's words to her mother-in-law—"For wither thou goest, I will go. Where you stay, I will stay. Your people shall be my people, and your Elohim my Elohim" (Ruth 1:16)—resound through history and across cultural boundaries. It is among the most universally recognized verse in Hebrew Scripture. Ruth surrendered to love. She did not operate from ego or fear. Ruth embodied the Shechinah's Sheltering Presence. Rabbi Lynn Gottlieb writes: "God in this story does not reveal Himself from a bush or a mountain or a dream or direct speech. Rather the presence of God is manifest through the love and caring of one woman for another."[22]

The name Ruth means "friendship." Friendship between women is a great blessing. Women's gift for relatedness is an expression of the Feminine Divine within us. It has the power to transform and sustains us throughout our days.

Simeon Solomon, *The Book of Ruth* (detail)

ESTHER
"Hidden One"
Ehstayr

King Ahasuerus, also called Xerxes, whose empire stretched from India to Ethiopia . . . 3 gave a banquet at his court. . . . 4 The festivities went on for a long time, a hundred and eighty days.

5 When this period was over the king gave another banquet for seven days, in the court of the palace garden, for all the people living in the walled city of Susa, from the humble to the great. 6 There were hangings of white and violet fastened to silver rings on alabaster pillars with cords of fine linen and purple thread and couches of gold and silver on a mosaic pavement of marble, mother-of-pearl and precious stones. 7 Royal wine in golden goblets was served in abundance, as befits a king. . . . 9 Vashti the queen made a feast for the women in the royal palace.

10 On the seventh day, when the king was merry with wine, he commanded seven eunuchs 11 to bring Queen Vashti to him wearing her royal crown, in order to display her beauty to the nobles, for she was a ravishing woman. 12 But Queen Vashti refused to come at the king's command, delivered by the eunuchs. The king became furious, his rage burned. . . . 17 The king's wiseman, Memucan, said, "The queen's conduct will soon become known to all the women, who will look with contempt on their husbands. They will say, 'King Xerxes himself commanded Queen Vashti to appear before him, but she would not come.'" . . .

19 "If it pleases your majesty, issue a royal decree. Let it be written into the laws of Persia and Media, that cannot be repealed, that Vashti is never again to enter the presence of King Xerxes. Give her royal position to a worthier woman. 20 Let this edict issued by the king be proclaimed throughout his vast empire, that all wives will henceforth bow to the authority of their husbands, high and low alike."

ESTHER : CHAPTER 2

2 The king's attendants proclaimed, "Let a search be made for beautiful young virgins for your majesty. 3 Bring them into the harem at the citadel of Susa, under the supervision of your eunuch, Hegai, guardian of the women. Give them beauty treatments, 4 and let the girl who pleases the king take Vashti's place as queen." This advice appealed to the king and he acted on it.

Theodore Chasseriau, *Esther at Her Toilet*

5 Now in the city of Susa lived a Jew named Mordecai. . . . 6 He had been driven into exile from Jerusalem by Nebuchadnezzar, the king of Babylon. 7 He was raising his niece, Hadassah, also called Esther. The girl was shapely and had a beautiful face. She had lost both mother and father. When her parents died, Mordecai adopted her as his own.

8 When the king's order was proclaimed, many maidens were brought to the fortress of Susa and entrusted to Hegai. Esther too was taken to the king's palace under the supervision of Hegai. 9 She pleased him and won his favor. Not only did he quickly provide her with beauty treatments and special food, but he chose seven maids—from the king's household—to serve her. He moved her and her maids to the best part of the harem.

10 Esther had not divulged her religion, because Mordecai had forbidden her to do so. 11 Every single day, Mordecai would walk up and down in front of the courtyard of the harem to find out how Esther was being treated.

12 Twelve months of beauty treatments preceded a girl's appearance before the king, six months with oil of myrrh and six months with perfumes and lotions. 13 When each girl went before the king, she could take anything she wanted with her from the harem into the king's palace. 14 She would go there in the evening and in the morning return to a second harem. . . . She did not go to the king again, unless he was particularly pleased by her and summoned her by name.

15 When it was Esther's turn, she asked for nothing beyond what Hagai recommended and won the admiration of all who saw her. 16 She was brought to King Xerxes in his royal apartments. 17 And the king loved Esther more than any of the other women. She won his approval and his kindness. So he crowned her queen instead of Vashti. 18 The king gave a great feast, Esther's banquet, for his princes and his servants. He declared amnesty on taxation and distributed gifts with royal liberality.

19 When the virgins were taken to the king's second harem, Mordecai was sitting at the palace gate. 20 But Esther did not acknowledge him. She kept her family background and religion secret, as Mordecai had instructed. For she continued to follow his advice as she had done when he cared for her.

21 While Mordecai was sitting at the king's gate, two of the king's guards, malcontents, became angry and plotted the assassination of King Xerxes.

22 Mordecai overheard them and told Queen Esther. Giving credit to Mordecai, Esther warned the king. 23 The matter was investigated and found to be true. The two malcontents were impaled on stakes, and the incident was written in the court archives in the king's presence.

refused to bow down because he was a Jew. 5 When Hamen saw that Mordecai would not kneel or bow down before him, he was outraged. 6 Having been told Mordecai's religion, Hamen scorned the idea of killing Mordecai alone. He made up his mind to destroy all of Mordecai's people, all the Jews in Xerxes' empire.

7 In the month of Nisan, dice (*pur*) were cast in the presence of Hamen, to select the day and month for the destruction of the Jews. 8 Hamen

ESTHER : CHAPTER 3

Shortly afterward, King Xerxes singled out Hamen for promotion and raised him to the highest rank. 2 All the courtiers knelt down and paid homage to Hamen, for the king had commanded this. Mordecai refused to bow down or prostrate himself.

3 "Why do you disobey the king's command?" the courtiers inquired. 4 Day after day they asked him, but he would not listen to them. They told Hamen about it, to see whether Mordecai's behavior would be permitted, because he had told them that he

said to Xerxes, "There is a certain people, scattered and dispersed among the others of your empire, whose laws are different from those of all other people, who do not obey the king's laws. It is not in your majesty's interest to tolerate them. 9 Let an edict be issued for their destruction. I will pay ten thousand talents of silver into the royal treasury for the men who will complete this mission." 10 The king took his signet ring from his finger and gave it to Hamen, the enemy of the Jews.

esther

11 "Keep the money," the king said, "and do whatever you want with the people." . . . 13 Instructions were sent by courier to all the king's provinces, with the order to destroy, kill and annihilate all the Jews, young and old, women and little children, on a single day—the thirteenth day of the month of Adar—and to seize all their possessions.

ESTHER : CHAPTER 4

When Mordecai learned what had happened, he tore his garments and put on sackcloth and ashes. He went through the city, wailing bitterly. . . . 3 In every province, when the edict came, there was great mourning, fasting, weeping and keening, and many lay in sackcloth and ashes.

4 When Queen Esther's maids and eunuchs told her about Mordecai, she was overcome with sorrow. She sent clothes for Mordecai to put on instead of his sackcloth, but he refused them. 5 So she summoned one of her eunuchs and sent him to Mordecai to ask what was grieving him and to find out why he was acting this way. . . .

7 Mordecai told him everything that had happened and about the money that Hamen had offered to put into the royal treasury to pay for the destruction of the Jews. 8 He also gave him a copy of the edict of extermination proclaimed in Susa for him to show Esther, with the message that she was to go to the king and plead with him for her people.

9 The eunuch came back and told Esther what Mordecai had said. 10 She answered with the following message for Mordecai: 11 "Everyone knows that for anyone, man or woman, to approach the king in his royal apartments without having been summoned, there is only one law. She must die, unless the king, by pointing his golden sceptre towards her, grants her life. Now thirty days have passed since I was last summoned to the king."

12 When Mordecai was told what Esther said, 13 he sent the following reply: "Do not suppose because you are in the king's palace, that you will be the one Jew to escape with your life. 14 No, if you keep silent at such a time, relief and deliverance will come to the Jews from another place, but both you and your whole family will perish. Who knows? Perhaps you have come to the throne for such a time as this."

15 Esther sent this message to Mordecai: 16 "Assemble all the Jews in Susa together and fast on my behalf. Do not eat or drink for three days and nights. I and my maidens will also keep the fast. Then I shall go to the king, in spite of the law, and if I perish, I perish."

ESTHER : CHAPTER 5

On the third day, Esther put on her royal robes and stood in the inner court, opposite the king's hall. The king was sitting on his throne facing the entrance. 2 When he saw Queen Esther standing in the court he was very pleased with her. He held the golden sceptre out to her. She came to him and touched the tip of his sceptre. 3 "What is troubling you, Queen Esther?" the king asked her. "Tell me what you want, even if it is half my empire, I grant it to you." 4 She replied, "If I have found favor in your majesty's eyes, please come and bring Hamen to a feast I have prepared for you."

Gregorio Pagani, *Esther before Ahasuerus* (Xerxes)

5 The king ordered, "Tell Hamen to come at once, so that Esther may have her wish." So the king and Hamen came to the feast that Esther had prepared. 6 As they drank their wine, the king said to Esther, "Tell me your request, I grant it to you. Tell me what you want, even if it is half my empire, it is yours for the asking."

7 "What do I want, what is my request?" Esther replied. 8 "If it please your majesty to grant my wish and agree to my request, let the king and Hamen come tomorrow, to a banquet I will prepare for them. Then I will answer you."

9 That day Hamen went out feeling joyful and elated. But when he saw Mordecai at the palace gate, and observed that he refused to stand or show fear in his presence, Hamen was furious at him. 10 However, he restrained himself. Returning home, he sent for his friends and Zeresh, his wife. 11 He bragged to them about his dazzling wealth, his many children, how the king had honored him and promoted him above the other nobles. 12 "What's more," said Hamen, "Queen Esther gave a feast, and did not invite anyone but me and the king. Better yet, she invited me and the king again tomorrow. 13 Yet all this means nothing to me, every time I see that Jew, Mordecai, sitting at the palace gate."

14 His wife and all his friends said to him, "Have a gallows built, fifty cubits high, and in the morning ask the king to hang Mordecai on it. Then you can go joyfully, with the king, to the banquet." Delighted with this suggestion, he had the gallows erected.

156

Hendrik met de Bles, *Esther and Ahasuerus* (Xerxes)

That night sleep deserted the king, so he called for the court archives to be brought and read to him. 2 It was written there how Mordecai had exposed the plot to assassinate King Xerxes. 3 "What honor and recognition was given to Mordecai?" the king asked. "Nothing at all has been done for him," his servants answered.

4 "Who is outside my chambers?" At that very moment, Hamen had entered the outer court to ask the king to have Mordecai hanged on the gallows he had just built. 5 "It is Hamen standing in the antechamber," the king's servants answered. "Bring him in," the king ordered. 6 When Hamen came in, the king inquired, "What should be done for a man whom the king wishes to honor?" Hamen said to himself, "Who would the king rather honor than me?" 7 So he said to the king, "If the king wishes to honor someone, 8 royal robes should be brought from the king's wardrobe, and a horse from the king's stable, wearing a royal crown on its head. 9 Let the robes and the horse be handed over to the noblest of the king's princes, who should dress the man whom the king wishes to honor and lead him on horseback through the city square, proclaiming, 'This is what is done for the man the king wishes to honor.'"

10 "Quickly," the king said to Hamen. "Go get the robe and the horse and do everything you have recommended for Mordecai the Jew." 11 So taking the robes and the horse, Hamen arrayed Mordecai and led him on horseback through the city square proclaiming, "This is what is done for the man the king wishes to honor."

12 Then Mordecai returned to the king's gate, while Hamen went hurrying home in misery, covering his face in grief. 13 He told his wife and friends what had happened. "You are beginning to fall, and Mordecai to rise," his wife, Zeresh, and his friends said. "If he is Jewish, you will not overcome him. With him against you, your fall is certain." 14 While they were still talking with him, the king's eunuchs arrived and hurried Hamen away to the banquet Esther had prepared.

ESTHER : CHAPTER 7

So the king and Hamen came to feast with Queen Esther. 2 On the second day, as they drank their wine, the king asked Esther, "Tell me your request, Queen Esther, I grant it to you. Tell me what you want, even if it is half my empire, it is yours."

3 "If I have found favor in your eyes, oh king," Queen Esther replied, "and if it pleases the king, grant me my life, that is my wish, and the lives of my people, that is my request. 4 For we have been sold, my people and I, to be destroyed, to be killed and annihilated." . . .

5 King Xerxes interrupted Esther. "Who did this?" he demanded. "Where is the man who thought of doing such a thing?"

6 Esther replied, "The persecutor, the enemy? Why this fiend is Hamen!" Hamen cringed in terror before the king and queen. 7 The king rose in fury, left the banquet and went out into the palace garden. When Hamen realized that the king had turned against him, he stayed to beg Queen Esther for his life.

esther

8 Just as the king walked in from the palace garden, into the banquet hall, he found Hamen sprawled across the couch where Esther was reclining. "What!" the king shouted. "Is he going to rape the queen in my own palace?" The words were scarcely out of his mouth, when a veil was thrown over Hamen's face.

9 One of the king's eunuchs spoke up, "Look, the very gallows that Hamen prepared for Mordecai, whose words saved the king, stand ready outside Hamen's house."

"Hang him on it," said the king. 10 So Hamen was hanged on the gallows he had erected for Mordecai, and the king's wrath subsided.

Jan Havickez Steen, *The Wrath of Ahasuerus* (Xerxes)

ESTHER : CHAPTER 8

That very day, King Xerxes gave Queen Esther the property of Hamen, the enemy of the Jews. Mordecai came before the king, for Esther had revealed how he was related to her. 2 The king slipped off his ring, which he had reclaimed from Hamen, and gave it to Mordecai. And Esther put Mordecai in charge of Hamen's property.

3 Esther pleaded with the king again, falling at his feet and weeping. She begged him to put an end to the evil plotted by Hamen against the Jews. 4 The king extended his golden sceptre to her and Esther stood up and faced him. 5 "If it pleases the king and I have won his favor," she said, "if my petition seems proper to him, may he issue a written proclamation revoking the dispatches Hamen had written, ordering the destruction of the Jews in all the king's provinces. 6 For how can I bear to see my people suffer? How can I bear witness to the extermination of my family?" . . .

10 Letters written in the name of King Xerxes and sealed with the king's signet ring, were sent by couriers riding horses from the king's own stud farms. 11 In them the king granted the Jews, in each and every city of his empire, the right to assemble and protect themselves. . . . 13 Copies of the text of this edict were issued as law in every single province, publicly displayed to all the people, so that the Jews would be ready to avenge themselves on their enemies. 14 The couriers, mounted on royal steeds, raced out with urgency at the king's command. The edict was proclaimed in Susa, the capital. 15 Mordecai left the king's presence in royal robes of cobalt blue and white,

with a magnificent crown of gold and a violet cloak of fine linen. The city of Susa shouted for joy. 16 For the Jews there was light and gladness and joy and honor. 17 In every province, and in every city, wherever the king's command and decree arrived, there was happiness and exultation among the Jews, with feasting and holiday making. Of the country's population many became Jews, because now the Jews were feared.

ESTHER : CHAPTER 9

On the thirteenth day of the twelfth month, Adar, the day in which the enemies of the Jews had hoped to crush them, the opposite happened. The Jews gained control over those who hated them. 2 In their towns throughout the provinces of King Xerxes' empire, the Jews assembled to strike at those who had planned to injure them. No one resisted, because they feared Mordecai. 4 Indeed, Mordecai was powerful in the palace and his reputation extended through all the provinces; Mordecai grew steadily more powerful. 5 So the Jews struck at their enemy with the sword, slaying and destroying. And they did what they pleased with those who hated them. . . .

24 The enemy of all the Jews had plotted to destroy them and had cast the pur for their ruin and destruction. 25 But when Esther came before the king, he issued orders that the wicked scheme Hamen had devised against the Jews should be visited upon Hamen. . . .

28 These days are recalled and observed in every generation, by every family, in every province and every city. And these days of Purim shall never cease among the Jews, and the memory of them shall never perish among their descendants. ◎◎

esther

Queen **ESTHER** was the superstar of the Bible. She was named for Ishtar, goddess of love and war, and she embodied the Shekhina—the Hebrew Goddess—when she saved her people. Esther is admired as one of the great Jewish heroines and endures as a model of feminine power and beauty.

The Book of Esther is the last women's tale in the Bible, a story of Jewish survival in the face of annihilation. Written when the Jews were in exile from the holy land, Esther's novella addresses issues of the long-term survival of the people of Yah amid the nations. It tells how to keep Jewish identity and conscience alive. Esther was Persian on the surface and Jewish in her heart. Her tale teaches that sometimes it is best to hide being Jewish. It also tells us to risk everything to save our people.

Queen Esther was successor to Queen Vashti, an independent, strong-willed, and ravishing woman who was banished because she refused the king's command to display her beauty before his drunken nobles. Modern women admire Vashti's autonomy, but classic rabbinic commentary disparages her for disobeying her husband. Vashti's rebellion was overt. In contrast, Esther's strength lay in softness, strategy, and secrecy.

Destiny brought Esther to the secluded and political world of the royal harem. Necessity taught her how to survive there. During a year of beauty treatments, Esther was prepared in every way to pleasure the king. And after one night with Esther, the king chose her above all other women. Overnight, a beautiful Jewish harem girl, exiled and orphaned, became queen of the mightiest empire on earth.

Jean Francois de Troy, *The Toilet of Esther* (detail)

Esther risked her life when, unbidden, she approached the king to save her people. "Everyone knows that for anyone, man or woman, to approach the king in his royal apartments without having been summoned, there is only one law. She must die, unless the king, by pointing his golden sceptre towards her, grants her life." (Esther 4:11) Before Esther faced the king, she fasted for three days and bravely avowed: "Then I shall go to the king, in spite of the law, and if I perish, I perish." (Esther 4:15)

When Esther appeared before the king, her love for her people was met by his love for her. "When he saw Queen Esther standing in the court he was very pleased with her. He held the golden sceptre out to her." Erotic love is suggested with the next line, "She came to him and touched the tip of his sceptre." (Esther 5:2) There is no denying that Esther's beauty, seductive charm, and sexual allure gave her power over the king. Her sexuality as well as her faith and superb strategic skill prevailed. Her story honors women's sexual power. Genocide was averted by Esther's courage and by the love she inspired.

Bernard Cavallino, *Esther before Ahasuerus* (Xerxes)

Her name means "hidden." Esther embodied hidden power.
She was a treasured role model to Marrano women—Jews who practiced their
religion secretly after the Spanish Inquisition. The king asked her, three times,
to tell him her request so that he might grant it, but Esther kept her mission and
her religion to herself until the propitious moment. Then she saved her people.

The romantic, lushly detailed, and action-packed Book of
Esther is read on Purim, an early spring holiday that ritualizes the release needed
after winter. It is read from a scroll called a *Megillah,* a word that has crept into
American English. Most people understand that "making a Megillah" out of
something means making a big deal of it. Purim is a time of merriment. There
is masquerading, feasting, drinking, and partying. We are told to drink so much
that we can't tell the difference between Mordecai and Hamen. All associations
with Purim are fun except one. The "big deal" that underlies the holiday joy is the
message to beware: Villians determined to destroy all Jews lived in the past and
live today.

Hitler, modern-day's heinous incarnation of Hamen, understood
that Esther's story had the power to catalyze resistance. He ordered German
synagogues closed and barred during Purim and he forbade the reading of the
Book of Esther, calling it "a pack of Jewish lies."

There is no mention of the Divine in Esther's story, yet her
name is mentioned fifty-five times, more than any other woman in the Bible. In
her tale, the light of the Shechinah shone through one vulnerable and valiant
woman. The Book of Esther teaches us to act on our own behalf to secure divine
deliverance.

Like Ruth—the only other woman to whom a book of the
Scripture is dedicated—Queen Esther embodied qualities of many of the
foremothers who came before her. Esther incorporated the physical attractiveness
of Rachel and the hidden holiness of Leah. She acted with honor like Hannah. Her
timing was crucial to the survival of the Hebrews, as was Miriam's—the other
ancestress whose story took place entirely outside the Holy Land. Like Deborah,
she was a warrior woman of profound influence. Love was the redemptive force
in Esther's story, just as it was in Ruth's. Esther's story ends the Hebrew Bible,
leaving us with the sacred message that the Divine resides in love. ☺☺

acknowledgments

I prayed for this book. I thank dear God/dess, Infinite One, Shechinah-Adonai, for making this book happen and giving me the opportunity to spend a year and a half of my life immersed in the Bible, research, and the creative process.

Lena Tabori empowered me to do this. She became an instant friend for life when she moved to San Francisco in 1991. Lena invited me to work with her, doing research and screening proposals. Working with Lena demystified the world of publishing for me. Sitting on a grassy little hill one day, I poured my heart out to Lena. I told her, "If I could do just one book as wonderful as your book, *Love: A Celebration in Art and Literature,* I would feel that I had done something meaningful with my life." I thank her for loving and inspiring me. *Listen to Her Voice* was born from my friendship with Lena Tabori, and from my passion for Judaism, feminism, and art.

My undying gratitude goes to Karen Silver, a gracious, encouraging and effective editor, formerly at Chronicle Books, who helped me develop the vision of this book. Without her, this book would not exist. Sarah Malarkey completed the editorial process with kindness, care, and keen intelligence. She was wonderful and taught me a lot. And Kandace Hawkinson's editorial input was crucial to the completion of the manuscript. My gratitude also goes to Caroline Herter, publishing director at Chronicle Books, for her support.

The authors in my bibliography were my teachers and study partners. I thank them for their insight, clarity, and brilliance.

My treasured friend Marsha Heckman, dream agent and dream-weaver, was my help-mate from the days that this book was only a dream until its full-term delivery. She and Pat Brill faithfully shared this Bible journey with me as we read and edited every word of the Black Fire together.

Donna "Dee" Goldman's assistance with art research was invaluable. Theodore Feder, Claudia Goldstein, and the staff at Artists Resource Society were terrific, unfailingly helpful and patient throughout the process. I am also very grateful to Susie Friedman, Franz Gisler, Lucien Krief, Ruth Shamash,

Yael Gahnassia, Agnes Abecassis, Amir and Ruth Doron, Michelle Puleo at Superstock, Nikki LaBranche at Christie's Images, and Lori Franklin and Pernilla Pearce at the Bridgeman Art Library for their aid in art research. Thank you to Naomi Teplow for her beautiful calligraphy and to Pamela Geismar for the lovely book design.

I gratefully acknowledge the support of Richard Levenson, Mindy Flynn, Linda Sunshine, Linda Ferrer, Jalaja Bonheim, Marcia Falk, Avram Davis, Nan Fink, Estelle Frankel, David Cooper and the staff at Afikomen Books, Barbara Berk and Jerry Shapiro, Nancy Rothman, Donnell and David Campbell, Linda Andrews, Jay Rehor, Frank Rehor, Stefanie Endler, Ted Kugelman, Barbara Joan Tiger Bass and Larry Lajmer, Rashida and Marley Lovell, Carol Bidnick, Barbara Sonneborn and Ron Greenberg, Marcia Lippman, Victoria Brill, Pat Hanson, Judith and Stephen Bernat, Enid Futterman, Joyce Wadler, Leah Garchik, Bronnie, Bob, Holly, and Shari Roxenberg, Barbara Sturman, Mark Lemley, Floyd Heckman, Chris Craig, Erica De Marco, Valerie Andrews, Celia Goldman and Dr. Joan Westenholz at the Bible Lands Museum in Jerusalem, Ilana Brody, Yoshua and Edna Sobel, the Avrahami family, Lawrence Jarach, Mikyla Bruder, Melia Franklin, and my friends at Kibbutz Shamir. Thanks to Nitzhia Shaked for sharing her perspective with me. I'm grateful to the kind and brilliant Rachel Biale for her suggestions.

Sara Sasha Perl-Raver, *mamashana,* thank you for loving and believing in me, feeding me fabulous meals, and gracing my life with your strong, delightful, loving presence.

Most of all, I acknowledge my beloved mate, Marty Perlmutter. "You lift me up!" You are my Sheltering Presence. For your support every step of the way, doing a trillion washes, vacuuming, putting my punctuation inside the quotation marks, reading every word in draft after draft, and sharing my life, I thank thee.

endnotes

1 Rabbi Joseph Telushkin, *Biblical Literacy* (New York: William Morrow, 1997), p. 9.

2 Rabbi Shoni Labowitz, *Miraculous Living* (New York: Simon and Schuster, 1996), p. 56.

3 Judith S. Antonelli, *In the Image of God: A Feminist Commentary on the Torah* (Northvale, New Jersey: Jason Aronson, 1995), p. 28.

4 Tamar Frankiel, *The Voice of Sarah* (San Francisco: HarperSanFrancisco, 1990), p. 86.

5 Esther Harding, *Woman's Mysteries Ancient and Modern* (New York: Harper Colophon, 1971), p. 127.

6 Raphael Patai, *The Hebrew Goddess* (Detroit: Wayne State University Press, 1990), p. 39.

7 Norma Rosen, *Biblical Women Unbound* (Philadelphia: Jewish Publication Society, 1996), p. 113.

8 Merlin Stone, *When God Was a Woman* (New York: Barnes and Noble Books, 1993), p. 154.

9 Judith Antonelli, *In the Image of God: A Feminist Commentary on the Torah* (Northvale, New Jersey: Jason Aronson, 1995), p. 108.

10 Louis Ginzberg, *Legends of the Jews* (New York: Jewish Publication Society of America, 1956), p. 287.

11 Ginzberg, *Legends of the Jews*, p. 370.

12 Adin Steinsaltz, *Biblical Images* (Northvale, New Jersey: Jason Aronson, 1994), p. 93.

13 Judith Plaskow, *Standing Again at Sinai* (San Francisco: HarperSanFrancisco, 1990), p. 25.

14 Leila Leah Bronner, *From Eve to Esther* (Louisville, Kentucky: Westminster John Knox Press, 1994), p. 174.

15 Jonathan Kirsch, *The Harlot by the Side of the Road* (New York: Ballantine Books, 1997), p. 296, citing Cheryl J. Exum, "Fragmented Women: Feminist (Sub)versions of Biblical Narratives." First published in the *Journal for the Study of Old Testament,* supp. ser. 163 (Sheffield, England: JSOT Press, 1993), p. 174.

16 Timothy White, *To Catch a Fire* (London: Corgi Books, 1984), pp. 62 – 63.

17 Timothy White, *To Catch a Fire*, p. 332.

18 Rabbi Joseph Telushkin, *Biblical Literacy* (New York: William Morrow, 1997), p. 254.

19 Merlin Stone, *When God Was a Woman*, p. 188.

20 Carol A. Newsom and Sharon H. Ringe, eds., *The Women's Bible Commentary* (Louisville, Kentucky: Westminster John Knox Press, 1992), p. 104.

21 Edith Deen, *All the Women of the Bible* (New York: Harper and Row, 1955; reprint, San Francisco: HarperSanFrancisco, 1983), p. 131.

22 Rabbi Lynn Gottlieb, *She Who Dwells Within* (San Francisco: HarperSanFrancisco, 1995), p. 164.

bibliography

Alter, Robert, trans. *Genesis*. New York: W. W. Norton, 1996.

Amplified Bible. Grand Rapids, Michigan: Zondervan Publishing House, 1965.

Anderson, Sherry Ruth, and Patricia Hopkins. *The Feminine Face of God*. New York: Bantam Books, 1991.

Antonelli, Judith S. *In the Image of God: A Feminist Commentary on the Torah*. Northvale, New Jersey: Jason Aronson, 1995.

Baskin, Judith R., editor. *Jewish Women in Historical Perspective*. Detroit, Michigan: Wayne State University Press, 1991.

benShea, Noah. *The Word: Jewish Wisdom through Time*. New York: Villard, 1995.

Bialik, H. M., and Y. H. Ravnitzky, eds. *The Book of Legends*. New York: Schocken Books, 1992.

Bloom, Harold, and David Rosenberg. *The Book of J*. New York: Grove Weidenfield, 1990.

Bronner, Leila Leah. *From Eve to Esther*. Louisville, Kentucky: Westminster John Knox Press, 1994.

Buchmann, Christina, and Celina Spiegel, eds. *Out of the Garden: Women Writers on the Bible*. New York: Fawcett, 1994.

Comparative Study Bible/King James Version, Grand Rapids Michigan: Zondervan, 1984.

Deen, Edith. *All of the Women of the Bible*. New York: Harper and Row, 1955; reprint San Francisco: HarperSanFrancisco, 1983.

Falk, Marcia. *The Book of Blessings*. San Francisco: HarperSanFrancisco, 1996.

Fox, Everett. *The Five Books of Moses*. New York: Schocken Books, 1995.

Frankel, Ellen. *The Five Books of Miriam*. New York: Grosset/Putnam, 1996.

Frankiel, Tamar. *The Voice of Sarah*. San Francisco: HarperSanFrancisco, 1990.

Ginzberg, Louis. *Legends of the Jews*. 3 vols. Philadelphia: The Jewish Publication Society of America, 1909.

Gottlieb, Rabbi Lynn, *She Who Dwells Within*. San Francisco: HarperSanFrancisco, 1995.

Gottwald, Norman K. *The Hebrew Bible: A Socio-Literary Introduction*. Philadelphia: Fortress Press, 1985.

Harding, Esther. *Woman's Mysteries Ancient and Modern.* New York: Harper Colophon, 1971.

Henry, Sondra, and Emily Taitz. *Written Out of History: Our Jewish Foremothers.* New York: Biblio Press, 1990.

Hirshfield, Jane, ed. *Women in Praise of the Sacred.* New York: Harper Perennial, 1994.

Hoffman, Edward, ed. *Opening the Inner Gates: New Paths in Kabbalah and Psychology.* Boston: Shambhala, 1995.

Hyman, Naomi M. *Biblical Women in the Midrash.* Northvale, New Jersey: Jason Aronson, 1997.

Kaplan, Rabbi Aryeh. *The Living Torah.* New York: Moznaim, 1981.

Kates, Judith A., and Gail Twersky Reimer. *Reading Ruth.* New York: Ballantine Books, 1997.

Kenton, Warren. *Kabbalah: The Divine Plan.* New York: Harper Collins, 1996.

Kirsch, Jonathan. *The Harlot by the Side of the Road.* New York: Ballantine Books, 1997.

Labowitz, Rabbi Shoni. *Miraculous Living.* New York: Simon and Schuster, 1996.

Lockyer, Herbert. *All the Women of the Bible.* Grand Rapids, Michigan: Zondervan, 1995.

Matt, Daniel C. *The Essential Kabbalah.* New York: HarperCollins, 1995.

Miles, Jack. *God: A Biography.* New York: Alfred A. Knopf, 1995.

Mitchell, Stephen. *Genesis: A New Translation of the Classical Biblical Stories.* New York: HarperCollins, 1996.

Moyers, Bill. *Genesis: A Living Conversation.* New York: Doubleday, 1996.

Nachman of Breslov, Rebbe. *The Empty Chair.* Woodstock, New York: Jewish Lights Publishing, 1994.

New American Standard Version. La Habra, California: The Lockman Foundation, 1977.

New Jerusalem Bible. New York: Doubleday, 1990.

New Revised Standard Version. Grand Rapids, Michigan: Zondervan Publishing House, 1996.

Newsom, Carol A., and Sharon H. Ringe, eds. *The Women's Bible Commentary.* Louisville, Kentucky: Westminster/John Knox, 1992.

Ochs, Vanessa L. *Words on Fire.* Orlando, Florida: Harcourt Brace, 1990.

Ostriker, Alicia Suskin, *The Nakedness of the Fathers.* New Brunswick, New Jersey: Rutgers University Press, 1994.

Patai, Raphael. *The Hebrew Goddess*. Detroit, Michigan: Wayne State University Press, 1994.

Petsonk, Judy. *Taking Judaism Personally*. New York: Free Press, 1996.

Pitzele, Peter. *Our Fathers' Wells*. New York: HarperCollins, 1996.

Plaskow, Judith. *Standing Again at Sinai*. San Francisco: HarperSanFrancisco, 1990.

Rosen, Norma. *Biblical Women Unbound*. Philadelphia: Jewish Publication Society, 1996.

Rosenblatt, Naomi H. *Wrestling with Angels*. New York: Delacorte Press, 1995.

Ruether, Rosemary Radford. *Womanguides*. Boston: Beacon Press, 1996.

Sheres, Ita. *Dinah's Rebellion: A Biblical Parable for Our Time*. New York: Crossroad, 1990.

Steinsaltz, Adin. *Biblical Images*. Northvale, New Jersey: Jason Aronson, 1994.

Stone, Merlin. *When God Was a Woman*. New York: Barnes and Noble Books, 1976.

Tanakh: The Holy Scriptures. Philadelphia: Jewish Publication Society, 1985.

Telushkin, Rabbi, Joseph. *Biblical Literacy*. New York: William Morrow, 1997.

Teubal, Savina J. *Sarah the Priestess*. Athens, Georgia: Swallow Press, 1984.

Trible, Phyllis, et al. *Feminist Approaches to the Bible*. Washington, D.C.: Biblical Archaeology Society, 1995.

Visotzky, Burton L. *The Genesis of Ethics*. New York: Crown, 1996.

Weissman, Rabbi Moshe, ed. *The Midrash Says*. New York: Benei Yakov Publications, 1980.

White, Timothy. *To Catch a Fire*. London: Corgi Books, 1984.

Winter, Miriam Therese. *Woman Wisdom*. New York: Crossroad, 1991.

The Woman's Study Bible. Memphis, Tennessee: Thomas Nelson, 1995.

Zornberg, Avivah Gottlieb. *The Beginning of Desire*. New York: Image Books, 1996.

list of illustrations

Courtesy of ART RESOURCE, NY: page 17: *Creation of Eve* by Andrea del Minga. Nimatallah/Art Resource, NY; Galleria Palatina, Palazzo Pitti, Florence, Italy; page 23: *She Shall Be Called Woman* (c. 1875–92) by George Frederick Watts. Tate Gallery/Art Resource, NY; Tate Gallery, London, Great Britain; page 27: *Abram's Counsel to Sarai* by James Tissot. Jewish Museum/Art Resource, NY; Jewish Museum, New York, NY; page 55: *Dante's Vision of Rachel and Leah* (1855) by Dante Gabriel Rosetti. Tate Gallery, London/Art Resource, NY; Tate Gallery, London, Great Britain; page 61: *Story of Jacob: Going to Canaan* by Raphael. Scala/Art Resource, NY; Logge, Vatican Palace, Vatican State; pages 76–77: *Tamar is Led to the Stake* (1566–67) by Jacopo Bassano. Erich Lessing/Art Resource NY; Kunsthistorisches Museum, Gamaeldegalerie, Vienna, Austria; page 94: *Jael Smote Sisera and Slew Him* by James Tissot. Jewish Museum/Art Resource, NY; page 113: *Meeting of David and Abigail* by Nicolas Vleughels. Scala/Art Resource, NY; Hermitage, St. Petersburg, Russia; page 119: *David and Bathsheba* (1562) by Jan Massys (1508–1575). Wood, 162 x 97 cm. Erich Lessing/Art Resource, NY; Louvre, Dpt. des Peintres, Paris, France; page 120: *The Prophet Nathan Admonishes King David* by Palma Giovane and workshop (Giacomo Negretti) (1548–1628). Erich Lessing/Art Resource, NY; Kunsthistorisches Museum, Gamaeldegalerie, Vienna, Austria; page 124: *Bathsheba* by Marc Chagall. Giraudon/Art Resource, NY. Copyright © ARS, NY. Private Collection, Basel, Switzerland; page 141: *Naomi entreating Ruth and Orpah to return to the Land of Moab* by William Blake. Erich Lessing/Art Resource, NY; Victoria and Albert Museum, London, England; page 142: *The Story of Ruth: Ruth and Boaz* (1876–77) by Thomas Matthews Rooke. Tate Gallery, London/Art Resource, NY; page 151: *Esther at Her Toilet* by Theodore Chasseriau. Erich Lessing/Art Resource, NY; Louvre, Paris, France; page 155: *Esther before Ahasuerus* (generally identified as Xerxes I) by Gregorio Pagani. The Book Esther is used as a legend for the Purim festival; it tells the story of the deliverance of the Jews under Ahasuerus, who made Esther his queen. Erich Lessing/Art Resource, NY; Kunsthistorisches Museum, Gamaeldegalerie, Vienna, Austria; page 156: *Esther and Ahasuerus* by Hendrik met de Bles. Scala/Art Resource, NY; Pinocoteca Nazionale, Bologna, Italy; page 162: *Esther before*

Ahasuerus by Bernard Cavallino (1622–54). Scala/Art Resource, NY; Uffizi Gallery, Florence, Italy.

Courtesy of the **BRIDGEMAN ART LIBRARY INTERNATIONAL LTD.**: page 49: *Jacob's Ladder* by William Blake (1757–1827). British Library, London/Bridgeman Art Library, London/New York; page 57: *Rachel at the Well* (1903) by Harry Mileham (1873–1957), Private Collection/Bridgeman Art Library, London/New York; page 87: *The Finding of Moses by Pharaoh's Daughter* (1904) by Sir Lawrence Alma-Tadema (1836–1912). Private Collection/Bridgeman Art Library, London/New York; page 93: *Barak and Deborah* by Francesco Solimena (1657–1747). Private Collection/Bridgeman Art Library, London New York; page 127: *The Queen of Sheba* by Rudolf Ernst (1854–1932). Whitford & Hughes, London/Bridgeman Art Library, London/New York; pages 130–31: *The Queen of Sheba before King Solomon* (1543) by Tintoretto (Jacopo Robusti) (1518–94). Kunsthistorisches Museum, Vienna/Bridgeman Art Library, London/New York; page 133: *Jezebel* (1896) by John Byam Liston Shaw (1872–1919). Russell-Cotes Art Gallery and Museum, Bournemouth/Bridgeman Art Library, London/New York; page 135: *King Ahab's Coveting: Ahab and Jezebel* (1879) by Thomas Matthews Rooke (1842–1942). Russell-Cotes Art Gallery and Museum, Bournemouth/ Bridgeman Art Library, London/New York; page 138: *King Ahab's Coveting: Ahab and Jezebel, Jezebel thrown to her death by two eunuchs, on the order of Jehu* (1879) by Thomas Matthews Rooke. Russell-Cotes Art Gallery and Museum, Bournemouth/ Bridgeman Art Library, London/New York; page 148: *The Book of Ruth* by Simeon Solomon (1840–1905). Private Collection/Bridgeman Art Library, London/New York; pages 152–53: *The Story of Esther* by Peter Witte (Peter Candid) (1548–1628). Roy Miles Gallery, 29 Bruton Street, London W1/ Bridgeman Art Library, London/New York; page 158: *The Wrath of Ahasuerus* (c. 1670) by Jan Havickez Steen (1625/26–79). The Barber Institute for Fine Arts, University of Birmingham, Great Britain/Bridgeman Art Library, London/New York; page 161: *The Toilet of Esther* (1738) by Jean Francois de Troy (1679–1752). Oil on canvas. Louvre, Paris, France/Bridgeman Art Library, London/New York.

Courtesy of **THE CLEVELAND MUSEUM OF ART**: page 66: *Laban Searching for His Stolen Gods* (early 1600s) by Bartolomé Estaban Murillo, Spanish (1618–1682). Oil on canvas, 243 x 362 cm. © The Cleveland Museum of Art, gift of The John Huntington Art and Polytechnic Trust.

Courtesy of CHRISTIE'S IMAGES, NEW YORK, LONDON:
pages 18–19: *Adam and Eve in Paradise* by Jan Brueghel and Peter Paul Rubens.
Mauritshuis, The Hague, Bridgeman Art Library/Christie's Image's; page 28: *Sarah Presenting Hagar to Abraham* by follower of Matthias Stommer; page 32: *Hagar Giving Ishmael Water from the Miraculous Well in the Desert* by Charles-Paul Landon (1760–1826); page 42: *Rebecca* by Arthur Reginald, reproduced by kind permission of Richard Green, photo courtesy of Christie's Images; page 69: *A Classical Beauty by a Well* by William A. Bouguereau (1825–1905); page 80: *Veiled Circassian Lady* by Jean Leon Gerome.

Courtesy of the CORCORAN GALLERY OF ART, WASHINGTON, D.C.: cover & page 41: *Rebecca at the Well* (1852) by Thomas Rossiter. Oil on canvas. Gift of William Wilson Corcoran.

Courtesy of DETROIT INSTITUTE OF ARTS: page 115: *The Meeting of David and Abigail* (1625/1628) by Peter Paul Rubens (and assistants). Gift of James E. Scripps. Photo copyright © 1984, Detroit Institute of Arts.

Courtesy EMB-SERVICE FOR PUBLISHERS, LUCERNE, SWITZERLAND: page 31: *Expulsion of Hagar* by Adrien van der Werfft (1659–1722); page 109: *Hannah brings her little son Samuel to Eli the priest* by Franck W. W. Topham (1838–1924). Mary Evans Picture Library, London.

Courtesy of the FINE ARTS MUSEUMS OF SAN FRANCISCO: page 64: *Jacob and Rachel at the Well* (c. 1680) by Johann Karl Loth. Museum purchase, M. H. de Young Memorial Museum, 47.9.

Courtesy of THE HARVARD UNIVERSITY ART MUSEUMS, THE FOGG ART MUSEUM: GRENCILLE L. WINTHROP BEQUEST: frontispiece: *The Days of Creation: The Sixth Day: Creation of Adam and Eve* by Sir Edward Burne-Jones.

Courtesy of the MUSEUM OF FINE ARTS, BOSTON: page 24: *Expulsion from the Garden of Eden* by Thomas Cole. Gift of Mrs. Maxim Karolik for the M. and M. Karolik Collection of American Paintings, 1851–1865.

Courtesy of THE NORTON SIMON FOUNDATION, PASADENA, CA.: page 51: *Rebecca at the Well* (1839) by Jean-Baptiste Camille Corot, French (1796–1875).

Courtesy of SUPERSTOCK, JACKSONVILLE, FLORIDA:
page 44: *Encounter between Rebeccca and Isaac* by Andrea Vaccaro (1598–1670);
page 75: *Judah and Tamar* by Emile Jean Horace Vernet; pages 84–85: *The Song of Miriam the Prophetess* by William Gale (1823–1909). Christie's Images/ Superstock; page 90: *Miriam Shut Out of the Camp* by James Tissot (1836–1902). Jewish Museum, New York/Superstock; page 98: *Deborah's Song* by Gustave Paul Dore (1823–83); page 101: *Samson and Delilah* by Peter Paul Rubens (1577–1640). National Gallery, London/Bridgeman Art Library, London/ Superstock; page 104: *Samson and Delilah* by Paul-Albert Rouffio (1847–1911). Musée des Beaux-Arts, Marseille, France/A.K.G. Berlin/Superstock; page 107: *High Priest and Hannah* by James Tissot (1836–1902). Jewish Museum, New York/Superstock.

Courtesy of YAEL GAHNASSIA, MAYANOT GALLERY, 28 KING GEORGE STREET, JERUSALEM, ISRAEL. TEL: 972-2-625 09 16 FAX: 972-2- 624 78 69: page 10: "Elohim remembered Rachel" by Abel Pann; page 37:"She laughed to herself" by Abel Pann; page 52: "Isaac playing with Rebecca" by Abel Pann; page 58: "Leah was weak-eyed" by Abel Pann; page 72: "Simeon and Levi . . . seized Dina from Shechem's house" by Abel Pann; page 83: "Every boy born of Israel must be thrown into the Nile" by Abel Pann.

Courtesy of the FAMILY OF Z. RABAN, JERUSALEM, ISRAEL:
page 144: *Boaz wakes to find Ruth at his feet* by Z. Raban; page 146: *Boaz pulled off his sandal* by Z. Raban.

bible
acknowledgments